NICK
MALLETT

THE STORY
SO FAR

Struik Publishers (Pty) Ltd
(a member of Struik New Holland Publishing (Pty) Ltd)
80 McKenzie Street
Cape Town 8001

Reg. No. 54/00965/07

ISBN 1 86872 201 5

First published in 1999
Copyright © in published edition 1999: Struik Publishers (Pty) Ltd
Copyright © in text 1999: Paul Dobson
Copyright © in photographs 1999: as credited on each page

Managing editor: Annlerie van Rooyen
Editor: Glynne Newlands
Design manager: Janice Evans
Designer and cover design: Sonia Hedenskog de Villiers
Proofreader: Alfred LeMaitre
Indexer: Gillian Gordon

Reproduction: Hirt & Carter Cape (Pty) Ltd
Printing: CTP Book Printers (Pty) Ltd, Caxton Street, Parow 7500, Cape Town

10 9 8 7 6 5 4 3 2 1

FRONT COVER Nick Mallett, Springbok coach (Tertius Pickard/Touchline
Photo Agency).
HALF-TITLE PAGE Training for the 1998 Tri-Nations Series (Dave Rogers/Allsport).
PAGES 4–5 Mallett playing for the Cape Barbarians in 1985 (source unknown).
BACK COVER On tour with the Boks (Tertius Pickard/Touchline Photo Agency).

AUTHOR'S ACKNOWLEDGEMENTS

When the English Rugby Union Writers' Club gives the South African rugby coach the award for rugby's outstanding personality of 1998, you know you are dealing with a special man. Nick Mallett is a special man, and he comes from a special family. It has been my special privilege to have known the Malletts from December 1965, when Anthony Mallett offered me a teaching post at the Diocesan College (Bishops). He was the best principal a schoolmaster and a school could have. At that time I first met Nick Mallett, a schoolboy.

Inevitably there are many people to thank. First of all there is Nick Mallett himself, for all that he has done for rugby and for being as open to the world as he has been. I have had particular and particularly generous help from his mother Vivienne, as well as from his wife Jane, his sisters Jenny, before her untimely death, and Tessa, his brother David and David's wife Karen.

Others who have been of help are my wife Margaret, as she always is, John Gardener as he always is, Douglas de Jager, who makes writing possible, Dennis Nick, by whose kindness I saw the Springboks in France and England in 1997, Tim Hamilton-Smith, Basil Bey, Ian and Viv Pinnington of Haileybury, Rex Pennington, Elizabeth Boardman, who is the archivist of Brasenose College, Kathy Drake of the South African Library, Stefanie Hudoffsky, John Dobson, Howard Bradshaw, Brian de Kock, the secretaries of Partick Thistle FC and Hibernian FC, Peter Golding, Peter Owens of the Welsh Rugby Union, Tim Brukman, Bob Bolus, Pippa Vintcent who is Fred Snell's daughter, David von Hirschberg, Joe Venter, Stoney Steenkamp, John Axe, Alan Douglas, Anthony Clark, Colin Douglas of the Scottish Rugby Union, Mrs Pat Ball and her son Anthony, Des Newton, David Jenkins of Bath, John Griffiths, who meticulously edits the *Rothmans Rugby Annual* each year, Rohan and Anthea Vos of Rovos Rail, Steve Leith, Tim Southey, Jean-Roger Delsaud, Sophia of the Italian Rugby Federation, Biddy Schalker of St Andrew's, Herman Jansen, Rob van der Valk, Alan Solomons, Professor André Odendaal, Dr Wayne Diesel, Jake White, Mike Bayly, Danny Hearn, Peter Dauncey, Gerald Alanthwaite, Jan Preuyt, Hennie Brandt, Dan Retief, Chris Danziger, Johan Kriel of *Die Burger* library, Mickey Gerber, Steve Griffiths of the International Rugby Board, Louis de Villiers, Linda Cousins of University College, Pat Hill of the Port of London Authority, Lew and Sue Byrne, Bevan Marchand of the Oxford University Bridge Club, Alan Zondagh, Nick Pagden, John Robbie, Ed Morrison, Ann McKinsley of the Edinburgh Reivers, Sonia Hedenskog de Villiers of Struik, Lisa Bon and Carla van der Merwe of SARFU, Paul Kumleben, Christine Williams, Ralph Kelly, John Jenkins, Anne Arkwright, André Homan, Peter Robinson and Dr Jean-Pierre Bodis of Pau.

Those who helped most in getting details right were Jean-Roger Delsaud, John Gardener, John Griffiths and the editor, Glynne Newlands, the kindest of ladies.

Lastly, I should like to thank Struik Publishers for asking me to write the book and, in particular, Alasdair Verschoyle and Annlerie van Rooyen. Photographs were largely the responsibility of Carmen Watts, much helped by Vivenne Mallett's collection.

PAUL DOBSON

DEDICATION

This book is dedicated with love, gratitude and admiration to Vivienne Mallett, and to the happy memory of Anthony, her husband, and Jenny her daughter who died so suddenly on 17 April 1999. It would be hard to equal or in any way estimate the loving support Jenny gave all members of her family, as daughter, sister and aunt – and her passion for rugby football.

CONTENTS

TOP: Nick, Tessa, Edith Harrison,
Jenny, Geoff and David Griffiths,
Anthony, Vivienne and David.
ABOVE: Anthony Mallett, and
pipe, at Peterhouse, 1963.
MIDDLE RIGHT: Nick and Jane at
their house in Greyton.
RIGHT: Nick, Kate and Dougie.

NICK'S FAMILY

Nick Mallett did not drop from the sky, a *deus ex machina* to save South African rugby. He was born into a certain family in a certain society. To understand something of his type of person, we need to know the family into which he was born, the type of society they inhabited, their ambitions and achievements, their education and activities.

The Malletts are a remarkable family, a family of achievers. And they are remarkable as a family in their cohesiveness and support of one another. They believe in family and live according to their beliefs. If you do not understand family, you cannot understand the Malletts, and you cannot understand Nick Mallett or much of the rationale behind his handling of his rugby team, his family-squad.

It is an emotionally supportive family, each one of all the others, each with a deep-rooted interest in the others' activities. Even with the death of the father of the family, Anthony Mallett, they remain united. No other bond surpasses their family-ness. What is surprising about this is that Anthony, the father of the family, was an only child. He was a man of unbounded energy and determination, but above all a team man, a family man.

ANTHONY

Anthony Mallett had many other beliefs besides strong religious ones. He believed in private (in England it is called public) school education, which he had himself enjoyed. He believed in the value of boarding school, which he had not experienced. He had a strong belief in community service and the energy, enthusiasm and principles to get a job done properly, whether it was gardening, teaching, speaking in public, coaching games, playing bridge or bird-watching. His son Nick would also claim to have been, all his life, a perfectionist.

Anthony's beliefs in family and education were simple, straightforward ones, based on goodness and a belief in the existence of goodness. His principles had a practical bearing on the way he acted himself and on behalf of his family. As he was a man of energy, conviction, focused concentration and powerful personality, his beliefs affected his sons and daughters profoundly.

Anthony William Haward Mallett was born in South London, at 148 Clive Road, Dulwich, on 29 August 1924, later moving to Beckenham. He was the only child of Wilfred Haward Mallett of the Metropolitan Water Board and Lucy Kathleen Mallett, née Honeysett. Father, who was usually known as Haward (pronounced Hoard), was a keen cricketer. Mother, called Kathleen, was an enthusiastic and good amateur actress. Wilfred Mallett also took part in amateur dramatics, usually as the butler or some such abbreviated rôle, and the three sometimes acted together. Father and son also sometimes played cricket together. Father was exemplary. Tired from work, he would change and take his son to nets or fielding practice. Young Anthony grew up enjoying both acting and cricket, both pursuits essentially requiring team work, both no doubt compensating for his only-child status. Anthony passed these interests and activities on to his son Nicholas. As his father spent time bowling and batting with him, so Anthony spent time bowling, batting and playing golf with Nick, and so Nick spends time bowling, batting and playing golf with his son, Dougie.

Those in England who believed in education tended to send their children either to public or grammar schools. Anthony enjoyed private school education throughout, first at St George's School, then at Clare House School (both in Beckenham) and then at Dulwich College during wartime.

An actor, Edward Alleyn, founded Dulwich in 1619. Unusually for a great English public school, it became primarily a day school, a large one of some 1 400 pupils. The college's best game has always been cricket, and AWH Mallett was amongst the very top cricketers who left the school.

In 1943 Anthony Mallett joined the Royal Marines and would have been launched into France on D-Day had he not broken his thumb boxing for the Marines. He went to France later. Apart from playing cricket for England in wartime internationals, he had also risen to the rank of lieutenant on discharge in 1946.

OXFORD

At school Anthony Mallett shone at cricket, squash, tennis and rugby, where he played at fullback. In 1947 he went up to Oxford on an army bursary. Dr William Stallybrass (William

Anthony Mallett was an excellent sportsman, and especially excelled at cricket. As a young man he played for Kent, the Gentlemen and the MCC.

MALLETT FAMILY COLLECTION

Teulon Swan Stallybrass), the principal of Brasenose College at Oxford, who was known as Sonners, was sympathetic to sportsmen and took Anthony Mallett in.

In the *Brazen Nose*, the college paper, there is a reminiscence dating back to 1946, in which a typical, apparently true, phone conversation between Stallybrass and an aspirant student was said to have run as follows:

> *Aspirant Student: I've just been demobbed and would like to come to Brasenose, Sir.*
> *Stallybrass (somewhat distantly): And what makes you think you should come here?*
> *Aspirant Student: I've played for the MCC, Sir.*
> *Stallybrass (with warm concern): My dear boy, where are you speaking from?*

BNC, as Brasenose is known in Oxfordese, was renowned amongst colleges as a refuge for sportsmen. At that time the MCC was cricket's highest authority, and it also chose teams. When official teams went abroad from England, they were known as the MCC, being called England only for test matches.

Mallett duly excelled at cricket and squash, for which he received Blues, the award for taking part in certain sporting contests with Cambridge. He was secretary of the Oxford squash club, and played squash for England and later for Rhodesia, as Zimbabwe was then called. And he also played tennis, table tennis, darts and bridge.

Of course, the sport was important, but he would have claimed that more important than that was his meeting with Vivienne Short, destined to play materfamilias to his paterfamilias. They met through sport but had come from different directions.

Anthony Mallett had had two excursions beyond South London – one to fight in Hitler's war and the other to Oxford after World War II. There he did a two-year degree for ex-servicemen subsidised by the state, something his father could not have afforded. He took his BA degree in English in December 1948 and was formally awarded it on 26 February 1949. His MA was awarded on 26 April 1956, a degree which conferred full membership of the university without any further study.

VIVIENNE

Vivienne Maud Short was born on 28 January 1928 in Peshawar, India, where her father, Vivian, was the head of the North West Constabulary. He had grown up on a sugar plantation on the island of Grenada in the West Indies but had been educated at Cranleigh School in England. Short was heading for retirement when Vivienne unexpectedly arrived – 16 years after her sister and 12 years after her brother, a *laatlammetjie* in South African parlance.

She was virtually an only child, by age and education. Her sister and her brother were too much older than she was for familiar contact. After the family returned from India to Bury St Edmunds in Suffolk, she had her parents' undivided attention, a situation fractured by World War II, for she was one of those evacuated to the USA and Canada. She travelled in a rickety ship that added seasickness to homesickness. It was a miserable time. Vivienne spent the years from age 11 to 14 in boarding schools in various places, including Chicago and Quebec. When she returned to England at the end of the war, she continued studying by correspondence.

As was the case with Anthony, this seemed inadequate preparation for her future rôle as materfamilias, not only of her tightly knit family but also of bigger families at schools. As a girl, she found it hard to get on with others. Coming as she did from a cosseted background, the 11-year-old Vivienne found it difficult to adapt to her peers, who seemed rougher and ruder, but she learnt the lesson of adaptability to avoid spending her youth condemned to isolation.

At home she worked harder than she needed to at her correspondence course and earned entrance to Oxford. Her father wanted her to read Maths, but she wanted to read English, which he thought was a waste of time. She wanted to be an actress, but her father put his foot down heavily and instead gave the rebellious 16-year-old the opportunity to do a secretarial course, either in London or Oxford. She chose Oxford.

Vivian Short had been a squash champion in India but he would not allow his daughter to play until she was 14 for fear of straining her heart. She played while in Oxford and was coached by the Oxford University coach who invited her to watch an exhibition match. There were two matches – one a women's match, and the marker was Anthony Mallett. They chatted, and he invited her to watch the men's match, in which he would be playing. She stayed and was astonished at the power of the players, but left before the end, lest she seem forward.

Anthony asked the Oxford coach for her address. He, trickster, gave the address of the captain of the Oxford women's team, who was certainly not Vivienne Short. Anthony Mallett wrote her a note, inviting her for tea and was surprised at the brawny lady who arrived. Anthony collared the coach who produced the address of the right girl, and this time the invitation started the love affair of a lifetime.

Beautiful, Vivienne Short was not yet 21 but had been in Oxford long enough to have enjoyed the company of many young men, particularly from Eton and Winchester. Impoverished, unaristocratic Anthony Mallett from Dulwich was different. He took her to dinner at an ordinary hotel. She wanted Pimms; he suggested shandy. He ended the evening with the cutlery spread all over the table to explain to her the various positions on a cricket field. She took him home to meet her parents, and her father took to Anthony immediately.

MARRIAGE

Anthony and Vivienne met in January 1948 and became engaged in July 1948. Anthony Mallett went down from Oxford in July of that year to teach at his old school, Dulwich, which he loved, but Vivienne stayed on in Oxford. On 20 August 1949, they married at St Michael's Church, Chester Square, Pimlico, London, with Canon FH Gillingham, a former Essex cricketer, to perform the ceremony. The best man, Tony Wortham, read only one telegram at the wedding reception – from DG Clark, the Kent captain, awarding Anthony his county cap. Anthony was 24, Vivienne 21.

The wedding was highly publicised, and much was made of Anthony's sporting prowess – 'the well-known Beckenham, Kent and Oxford University cricketer', who had 'twice represented the Gentlemen v. Players [he was never a professional cricketer] at Lords and played for England against the Dominions in wartime test matches'. The newspaper also reported that they would honeymoon at Braemar and then at Hastings 'where the bridegroom will play in Cricket Festival matches'. Cricket was important to Anthony. He had even written affectionate letters to his fiancée on paper emblazoned with the Beckenham Cricket Club letterhead. In 1951 he toured Canada with the MCC.

On the wedding list were Mr and Mrs Rex Pennington. The announcements of the engagements of Rex to Sarah and Anthony to Vivienne had been published in the same edition of *The Times*. Their paths ran together, diverged and converged. Rex, a Rhodes scholar from Michaelhouse in the former Natal, South Africa, was captain of squash in Oxford in 1948. He played number 1 and Anthony number 2. Rex was a housemaster at Bishops when Anthony was appointed principal there and in 1966 he became Anthony's vice-principal. The Malletts and Penningtons have remained close friends.

Shortly after their wedding, Vivienne's father became fatally ill with cancer, and to help in nursing him, the young couple moved from their flat in Flood Street, Chelsea, to Vivienne's parents' home on the Thames between Staines and Chertsey, which meant a lot of travelling for Anthony to get to Dulwich. Anthony, who was remarkably kind in caring for his father-in-law, was also destined to die of cancer. Vivian Short died on 21 July 1950.

Life in London was expensive and uncomfortable. Vivienne, who worked for Toc H (a service organisation founded by Rev. Tubby Clayton at Poperinghe in Belgium during World War I for servicemen of all ranks), was pregnant, and Anthony went for an interview at Haileybury, a fine and imposing public school in rural surroundings in Hertfordshire. The Malletts wanted to get out of London.

The new Mr and Mrs Anthony Mallett. They were married on 29 August 1949 at St Michael's Church in Pimlico, London.

MALLETT FAMILY COLLECTION

HAILEYBURY

Founded in 1862, Haileybury's buildings were originally those of the East India College, which in turn had been founded at Hertford Castle in 1806, moved to Haileybury in 1809 and closed in 1858. In 1942 the school became the Haileybury and Imperial Service College when the latter joined Haileybury.

Haileybury's roots were very much in the East India Company, which may have touched a chord in Vivienne Mallett, born in Peshawar in India. The prospect of Anthony and Vivienne's going to Haileybury greatly pleased Vivian Short, ill as he was. After all, Vivian's two nephews had been to Haileybury. Sir Pelham Warner, the most loved of cricket administrators and universally known as Plum, had suggested the idea and did much to smooth Anthony's way to Haileybury.

On 5 April 1950, Anthony Mallett received a 'Dear Mallett' letter from the Master (as the headmaster is called there) of Haileybury, Christopher Smith, offering him a teaching post for £310 per annum, which included recognition of war service and two years' teaching experience. Part of the deal was accommodation, initially above the music school (now called the Old Music School), for which rent of about £50 per annum was charged.

In September 1950, when the Malletts went to Haileybury, it was a boys' public school with 538 pupils in 11 houses, paying £225 per annum. In 1998 it became a co-educational school of 484 boys and 138 girls, paying £14 600 per annum for a boarder. Most of the pupils are boarders.

The Malletts loved Haileybury, as they did all schools at which they taught – Dulwich, Peterhouse, Bishops and St Joseph's in Rondebosch, Cape Town. They acquired their first dog at Haileybury – Tina, a spaniel, as most future Mallett dogs would be. (Later there was also a corgi and a Labrador.) Their first children, Jennifer Wilna Kathleen (her second and third names from her grandmothers) and Tessa Mary, were born there. They moved to a bigger house, and Nicholas Vivian Haward Mallett was born in Haileybury's Highfield Cottage, Dr Billingham's residence which had been turned into flats. The Malletts occupied the ground floor.

Danny Hearn, the former England rugby player who has long been on the staff at Haileybury, with his particular affection for South Africa, would show South African boys around the school. One of the sights he would show them was the Old Music School where 'Nick Mallett was born'. Some would be photographed outside it as if at a shrine. Only later he discovered it was not the right place after all.

Nick Mallett was born at Haileybury at 8 pm on 30 October 1956, a huge baby of 9$\frac{1}{2}$ lbs (4.3 kgs), whose birth was easier than the births of his sisters had been, though two weeks late. A doctor and a nurse were present. The Rev. Richard Thomas christened Nick in the Haileybury Chapel. His godmothers were Wilna Short, Vivienne's sister, Catherine Nurden, who was the wife of a Haileybury housemaster, and Imogen Thomas, who wrote a history of Haileybury up to 1958. His godfathers were Jack Thomas, Buddy Davis, and David Ramsbotham, whose gift to his godson was a recording of *Rule Britannia* and the promise of bottles of port for his 21st birthday, which never arrived. Ramsbotham was later an army general. Jack and Imogen Thomas were on the staff at Haileybury and close friends of the Malletts.

The fourth child, Anthony David, was born at Peterhouse in the then Rhodesia on 14 December 1959, 'easily and uneventfully', according to his father. They are all school children by birth. Jennifer is called Jenny, Tessa Tizzy, Nicholas Nick or Nicky and Anthony David or Dee. Vivienne referred to her husband as Ant though many of his contemporaries called him Tony. He always called his wife Vivienne. In his sermon at Anthony Mallett's funeral, the Rev. Bob Commin remarked that he found it strange that such a big man should be referred to by his wife as Ant!

The Malletts loved life at Haileybury. Anthony taught Latin and English, was master in charge of cricket, squash and boxing, coached rugby, acted in staff plays and was deputy housemaster of Trevelyan, directly across the quad from the Master's Lodge. They had enormous fun with other members of staff, especially the bachelors, but they were austere times and the Malletts were battling to make ends meet.

When Vivienne was pregnant with Nicholas, a cousin of hers, Buddy Davis, wrote from Salisbury in Rhodesia (now Harare in Zimbabwe) where he had settled to tell Vivienne's mother about a new school that was being founded – Peterhouse, at Marandellas – and wondered if Anthony was interested in a post there. Anthony wrote off, not with great enthusiasm. He sent the letter by ordinary mail and was probably relieved when there was no reply. Suddenly a telegram came from Fred Snell, the first rector of Peterhouse (previously rector of Michaelhouse). Off Anthony went to be interviewed by Frank Fisher, then at St Edward's in Oxford. Fred Snell invited Anthony to join the staff at Peterhouse. He hesitated, but Vivienne pressed him for a decision. She believes that the decision, when it came, may have been nudged to finality for a tiny consideration: at the time tobacco in Rhodesia was £5 a sack, an attractive proposition to Anthony with his vigorous pipe, especially as Vivienne found tobacco wastefully expensive in their circumstances.

The decision was made. Haileybury regretted the departure of the Malletts, and on 12 August 1956, Anthony Mallett received the following letter:

Dear Mallett,

I am enclosing a cheque which I ask you to accept as a help towards all the extra expense that you will be put to between now and the end of the year, in removing your stuff and booking passages and so on.

We have all deeply appreciated your services to Haileybury while you've been with us, and we'll miss you all as I expect you will also miss us. You know that I think you are doing the right thing, and I trust it will prove a triumphant success.

Please, accept this cheque as a token of friendship and goodwill. I send it in the hopes it will do something to lessen the anxiety you must naturally feel in facing added expenses at this time.

Yours ever
RLA [RLA was Robert Leslie Ashcroft, the second master]

Nicholas was hardly born when furniture was moved out, and on 21 December 1956 the family set sail from the West India Docks on a 6-week, nightmare journey on the Natal Line's *Umtali*, which was built in 1936 and had seen heavy duty in World War II. The Suez Crisis meant that they had to sail for Beira, in Mozambique, around the southerly tip of Africa. The ship was not in great shape and found sailing a strain, as did the passengers as the air conditioning and toilets kept breaking down.

On the voyage baby Nicholas contracted pneumonia. The aged doctor on board, who had not heard of penicillin, was not of great use, and the ship's nurse had them paint his throat with gentian violet, a mild antiseptic, an unpleasant experience for the little baby. In Cape Town Dr George Bradshaw came aboard. He was persuaded to look at the baby and recommended an antibiotic. In Port Elizabeth, Anthony found a chemist and Nicholas recovered.

The Malletts disembarked in Beira on 29 January 1957 and took the train for Salisbury. The journey from Beira certainly suggested that they were in 'real Africa' as they rocked their way up through the wild bush. On the train, a Portuguese boy played with the children, who got chickenpox from him, with which they in turn infected the whole of Peterhouse. The Malletts had arrived in Africa.

RHODESIA

Peterhouse, founded in 1953, was a new school of some 400 boys when the Malletts arrived in 1957. At the time an unimposing collection of low buildings, it is located outside a small town an hour or so's drive from Harare. It is on large property, sprawled about the bush, a wonderful place for children to grow up running free. The school remains proudest of its chapel, its grandest building.

Fred Snell, who had been made rector of Michaelhouse in then Natal (South Africa) at the age of 35, was the first rector of Peterhouse, which was much under the Michaelhouse influence, as the name suggests. The Malletts would always hold Snell in high regard – a man who backed his staff, gave them their heads, allowed them the praise if things went well and took the blame if plans went awry. Snell retired at Marandellas (which became Marondera after the country's independence), was secretary/treasurer for the Anglican Church in the Central African Province, retired in Borrowdale, Harare, and died in 1991 at the age of 87.

It was a different life for the young family from manicured England, and it took them a while to settle down. The sight of Nick with a partly devoured shongolola (a black millipede with a hard, shiny exterior) dangling from his mouth was certainly not an English sight!

Dr Danie Craven, South Africa's rugby legend, believed that rugby players were born and bred in the rural areas where they developed both physical co-ordination and confidence in their physical abilities. It also meant a great deal of self-reliance as bouts of loneliness were inevitable for a small boy in the country when sisters are at school, especially when they went off to board at nearby Bishopslea. When his father flew to

Jenny, Vivienne, Nick, Anthony and Tessa leave Cape Town for Southampton, 1959.

England to attend his own father's funeral in 1961, Nick missed him greatly and gave him a great welcome when he got home.

Nick learnt to swim by jumping into the pool at the age of two and sinking to the bottom, whence he was rescued. But he thought this a good idea and repeated it. Eventually his mother tied some rope about him and hauled him to the surface when she thought he had had enough of underwater swimming.

Just after Nick's third birthday the family went to Europe on the *Pendennis Castle* and returned on the *Capetown Castle*. He won prizes for fancy dress on both ships – as a boxer and as Noddy. The trip included skiing in Austria.

During the voyage Nick was bet £5 to swim the length of the pool. In he dived and soon came out livid. It was a saltwater pool and, swimming mostly underwater as he did, he could not open his eyes to see his way. In fact, he had difficulty even getting into the pool which he thought was a big hole in the ship and, swimming at the bottom as he preferred, thought he would land at the bottom of the ocean.

When Nick saw a red double-decker bus for the first time during their stay in London, he asked: 'Why has that bus got another bus on its head?'

MALLETT FAMILY COLLECTION

1963 and the Malletts' last morning at Peterhouse before leaving for Bishops.

Back in Rhodesia, Nick and his Peterhouse friend, Ewan Campbell, roamed freely, not always without mischief. On one occasion Vivienne came to the table to find that they had tipped her cottage pie onto the table, and built a mountain with valleys and rivers of tomato sauce. She banished them to Nick's bedroom. All was quiet, which caused her suspicion, and on investigation she found that they had gone out through the window. They were discovered in the new classroom block which was due to be opened. The boys had found purple paint and had taken a classroom each and proceeded to daub and flick them purple. The opening of the classrooms had to be delayed.

At Marandellas Nick had a donkey to ride, given to him by Sister Ursula from a nearby mission station. The donkey, whose name was Donk, preferred to go backwards. The only way it would go where Nick wanted it to go was when boys from Ellis House propelled it forward, sometimes virtually carrying it! When he was four, Nick phoned Fred Snell, the rector, and asked him to go and see if Donk was not perhaps grazing on the field, which confirmation would save Nick a journey. The rector was not greatly amused!

Then there were horses and fish, pigeons and rabbits. For his second birthday he was given something like 20 balls of different kinds. He would grow up playing with balls. In 1962, just before his fifth birthday, accident-prone Nick fell and a piece of khaki-weed went in his left eye. It left three splinters in the eyeball, which had to be removed. For a few years he looked studious in glasses in an effort to correct the 'lazy' eye, which indeed happened. While he was at Western Province Preparatory School (WPPS) in Cape Town he was still going for eye exercises three times a week until 1966, but luckily he started to benefit and to disprove the early diagnosis of permanent damage to the eye. According to Vivienne he broke on average two pairs of spectacles a week!

But then he was always a past master at breaking things, especially chairs. When he was four, the Malletts were at the Snells for a Christmas party. Nick saw Margaret Snell, of whom he was fond, out in the garden. He ran out to join her – through a plateglass window which shattered, cutting his stomach and knee. They wrapped him in a towel and rushed him off to the school's sanatorium. The matron attended to him, but she said afterwards that she thought in horror, on seeing the bloody towel, that Nicky had been cut in half and they had brought him to her to put him together again!

It was a characteristic that would remain part of Nick's life. As a university student, he came driving down Woolsack Road from the University of Cape Town (UCT), straight across the intersection and into a house, destroying his mother's car. But then his own, an ancient Anglia, had already been destroyed.

Nick may have been accident-prone but he maintained good friendships. One of his friends of longest standing is Pete Golding. They were at school together from Std I to post-matric, most of the time as boarders. In their student days Mallett and friends seldom thought of going home on a Saturday night without visiting the Goldings in Kent Road, Newlands (Cape Town). There it was never too late to party.

One night, Mallett was at the Goldings for a shipwreck party. At the end, clad solely in a towel, he and his girlfriend at the time, dressed only in a negligée, went to his Anglia, which had the annoying habit of starting with difficulty. It needed to be shoved and the big man would shove, partly behind, partly to the side and then dash forward and leap in when it took. After this particular party, the negligéed girlfriend got into the car while Mallett pushed. The car suddenly took, Mallett lost the towel around his waist and watched in horror as the car sped down the road to come to rest in a neighbouring garden. It was an embarrassing situation.

CHANGE COMETH

With his energy and zest, Anthony Mallett meant a great deal to Peterhouse, teaching Latin and English, coaching cricket and squash, and producing and acting in plays. Vivienne was even more active on the stage and won the trophy for the Best Actress in Southern Rhodesia in 1963. As housemaster of Ellis House (appointed in 1958) and then second master (appointed 1961), Anthony had a great opportunity to form the ethos of the new school.

Then Fred Snell told Anthony Mallett, of all people, that he was lazy, not applying for headmasterships. And so it happened that, in 1963, he applied to the Diocesan College (Bishops) in Rondebosch, 8 kilometres from the centre of Cape Town. His application was two months late, but he got the job. The family believed that the Bishops council was unable to make up its mind and was then relieved to get a new applicant and gave him the job. If that was the case it was a happy fault – for Bishops and for the Malletts.

Vivienne described their interview period at Bishops, which lasted five days, with unnecessary diffidence: 'As far as I could see, I wore the wrong clothes on every occasion – had swotted up world affairs and they only discussed the present renaissance of Italian art – and generally put my feet in things; so it says even more for Ant that they accepted him despite me!'

BISHOPS

The Diocesan College was founded in 1849 by Bishop Gray, the first Anglican bishop of Cape Town, at his house in Bishopscourt and was referred to as the Bishop's school or simply Bishops. It did not take long before the bishop restored tranquillity to his surroundings by moving the school to a property in Rondebosch which was regarded as barren and remote from the centre of the city. Initially the school struggled but started growing in 1861 when Canon George Ogilvie arrived from prosperous St George's Grammar School, which was then based at the Cathedral in Cape Town. He introduced his form of football that year and is regarded as the founder of South African rugby. Under him Bishops became a university college in an increasingly affluent suburb.

BISHOPS AND THE MALLETTS

Anthony's predecessor at Bishops had been Hubert Kidd, a scholarly and seemingly remote man who had been at the school for 42 years by 1963. He and his wife Mary were remarkably kind to the Malletts, getting them introduced to Bishops. Kidd, who had been the first layman to be headmaster of Bishops, did not live to see Anthony installed, for he died in King William's Town in October 1963.

Settling into Bishops – grand accommodation, flourishing school and splendid view of the mountains – was not easy for the Malletts because they hankered after Rhodesia and thought of themselves as Rhodesians. There was, however, the compensation of being away from the political upheaval and outright civil war in Rhodesia as it battled its way towards independence and the new Zimbabwe. But, typically of the Malletts, Bishops soon became absorbed into the family concept.

Vivienne read to new boys, and there was all manner of hospitality to the various constituents of the school – council, staff, old boys, visitors, cultural groups, sporting groups, cadet folk, houses and so on. They became the heads of an extended family and concerned themselves with all aspects of it. The 'family of Bishops' soon became a reality.

Although Anthony gardened with vast enthusiasm from the start of their marriage, none of this enthusiasm rubbed off on Nick. The new principal in his garden soon became one of the sights of Bishops – pipe in mouth, baggy khaki shorts and bare torso, prodding eagerly at a border of bright colours. There was even the occasion when, as prospective parents arrived, he dived flat on the ground and hid between rows of beans till they had gone past and he could slip into the house by the back door, clean up and see them. At times, visitors mistook him for the gardener.

Donald Macdonald, whose three sons, Dugald, Donald and Coll, won rugby Blues at Oxford (Dugald also played for South Africa, Donald for Scotland), provided the Malletts with a mountain retreat. The escape in the summer holidays was in Du Toit's Kloof where Donald had purchased a stretch of river to pursue his passion for trout fishing. Here there was a cottage perched across the river to which all provisions were carried, a braai place around which Anthony would plant petunias, a rock pool where the price of a swim was removing 20 rocks from the water, walks and picnic expeditions in the mountains and evening games of cards, acting and darts.

Throughout their marriage the Malletts managed good holidays, including a trip on Rovos Rail, a gift from a former Bishops boy and the owner of the train, Rohan Vos.

In 1963 Bishops had some 60 boys at the Pre-Prep, as the Nursery School was called, 180 at the Prep school and 370 (220 boarders and 150 day boys) at college. One of the changes in Anthony's time at Bishops was the change from predominantly boarding to predominantly day. When he came to Bishops there were three boarding houses and two day houses in the college. The school, even for day boys, was run as if it were wholly a boarding school. When he ended his stay in 1982, there were some 900 boys at Bishops, roughly 600 at college. Most of those at college were day boys and a third day house had been added, Kidd House, named after Hubert Kidd.

The Malletts' regime – for it is best to record that running Bishops was a combined effort for Anthony and Vivienne – was a time of building and development. Anthony, who really believed in education, especially private school education, believed that boarding school was good, and so his children boarded.

EDUCATING THE FAMILY

Before he was four, Nick Mallett started at Peterhouse Nursery School, an initiative of staff wives led by Mrs Snell, and then moved on to Springvale School, a primary school

MALLETT FAMILY COLLECTION

attached to Peterhouse. In 1963 Anthony Mallett was appointed principal of Bishops. Schooling for his son would be a problem for the new principal.

Jenny, at this stage, was at Roedean in Johannesburg. She finished her schooling there, loved the school and was a prefect in her matric year. In Cape Town, Tessa would go to Herschel and was then intended for Roedean, which did not happen.

There was not an easy equivalent for Nick, who had been put down for Haileybury at birth and would have started there in 1970. It did not seem

A bespectacled Nick Mallett in 1963. He broke on average two pairs of glasses a week!

right that he should go to Bishops' rivals such as Rondebosch, 400 metres away, or SACS, both excellent schools but neither of them private – and the principal of Bishops would be expected to support private schools. Bishops had its own prep school but it would be tough for the boy to be at his father's school. And so he went into boarding school. Springvale in his last term of 1963 was a trial run. Nick Mallett boarded for the rest of his schooling, first at Western Province Preparatory School (WPPS) in Claremont, Cape Town, and then at St Andrew's College in Grahamstown.

Jenny thrived as a boarder, Tizzy hated it and became a daygirl while at Herschel, Nick put up with it as a necessity and did well from it, and David also hated it. To be fair, David did not like school and even at Miss Williams's nursery school he rebelled. The experienced Miss Williams decided that he was 'a challenge'. But schools and teaching stayed close to the Malletts. Jenny, who managed the Western Province schools hockey team while at UCT, taught, put on plays, coached rugby and became a school principal of St George's Preparatory School; Nick set out to be a teacher, enjoyed a taste of it at Fairmont and ended up a coach, which is merely another form of teaching; and David became a schoolmaster and the eighth headmaster of Western Province Preparatory School, his old school, and joined the board of governors of St Andrew's College.

Understanding this strong, aggressively united, emotion-charged family that went beyond the family members to include the whole of the Mallett activity, is important in understanding Nick Mallett's relationship with and treatment of his family-team, the Springboks.

Fred Allen (the former All Black captain and famous coach of the All Blacks), said of coaches: 'They are seldom satisfied, seldom happy and seldom at home.' As a professional coach Nick Mallett would have longer periods of time at home than most working men but also longer periods of time away. Weekdays had more freedom, weekends less, but it was not just the time spent coaching that dragged him from home. The emotion and absorption in coaching took him away even when he was at home, and there were also promotions and time spent preparing for trips. Mallett calculated that in 1998 he was away from home for some five to six months all told, what with the Super 12, Tri-Nations, recces, coaching clinics, sponsors' functions and promotional demands.

In 1999 things will be no different.

Recces to investigate hotels and facilities are important and led, for example, to a change of hotel from Perth to Fremantle in 1998. The South African Rugby Football Union (SARFU) requires that the coach be available for 12 promotional activities a year – such as attending the announcement of South African Airways (SAA) as one of the four elite sponsors of the Rugby World Cup in 1999, helping with Child Welfare on Red Nose Day and attending coaching clinics in Cape Town, Port Elizabeth, Durban and Pretoria to give local coaches the opportunity to learn how the Springboks do things. These clinics also aim to identify talented players.

Whenever Mallett attended such things he would give of his energetic best, as his nature demanded.

HIS OWN FAMILY

1978 was to be a good year: he and Jane Whipp started going out. Jane Olive Whipp, daughter of John and Joan Whipp, had known Nick from childhood, for she would go along with her parents to watch her brother Peter play cricket or rugby at Bishops. Peter, who left Bishops in 1968, was an excellent sportsman, a Nuffield cricketer who was unlucky not to have made the South African schools team, a Springbok rugby centre of the most creative kind and a good athlete.

Jane started her UCT career at Ballet School and then went on to do a BA, which she finished when Nick was studying at Oxford. She stopped her performer's diploma early because she had already been accepted by CAPAB (the Cape Performing Arts Board).

The one person on earth who can keep Nick's feet on the ground is Jane. Come back from Tri-Nations with a great win and a head full of confidence and Jane will put it into perspective. Be loudly determined and a quiet voice will say: 'I understand, Nick, darling, but the answer is No.'

When Karen, before she married Nick's brother Dave, was having problems in the relationship, she sought a sympathetic ear from Nick, who said: 'Karen, you must remember one thing – you can never change a man.' Nick may not have changed but he does not always get his own way either.

MARRIAGE

Nick and Jane were married in Christ Church, Constantia, by the Rev. Ian Eve on 24 February 1984. The best man was Tim Brukman, the groomsman Dave Mallett and the bridesmaids Jackie Salton and Adell Phillipson.

The St George's Preparatory School choir sang, but when it got to singing *Guide me, O thou great Redeemer*, the congregation, many of whom were rugby players, took it away on their own, regardless of the organist.

The reception was held in the cellar behind Groot Constantia and Peter Whipp was the master of ceremonies. It was a wonderful party, attended by rugby players and ballet friends and friends of both families, and the young couple thoroughly enjoyed it, only getting away at something like 1 am.

MALLETT FAMILY COLLECTION

The first night of their honeymoon was to be spent at Houwhoek Inn, in the mountains beyond Elgin on the way to Hermanus. They arrived to find the place locked and in darkness. A big wind blew, like a scene from *Wuthering Heights*. Eventually Nick found a sleeping night porter who opened the hotel for them. It was quarter to three in the morning when the bridal couple reached their nuptial bed.

The rest of their honeymoon was spent in Plettenberg Bay and Knysna.

CHILDREN

Both their children were born in France when they were living in Saint-Claude, a small town near the Swiss border when Nick was player/coach to the local club:

Kate Jennifer Mallett, born 13 February 1987;

Douglas John Haward Mallett, born 2 February 1989.

Nick Mallett is most secure in the peaceful, quiet and happy activities of his own family. He believes that he steps out of the limelight easily to become a husband and a family man. Jane keeps the children cared for and well adjusted while their father is away. She keeps Nick well adjusted when he returns home in triumph. She supports him, levels his euphoria and lifts his black moods. She takes him away from rugby. They go to the

MALLETT FAMILY COLLECTION

movies, she introduces him to new books and they take holidays in Knysna, St Francis and, in September 1998, at Etosha Pan.

For the family, the pressure and the absences were initially tough as their father was launched into stardom. For Jane, who shuns limelight, this was especially true. But gradually the enormity of the change subsided, the novelty wore off and the family adapted. They became a normal family. Nick was good, making long phonecalls home to his children, but they missed him. For Dougie there was no more cricket on the lawn! Luckily for them, Nick, despite the outward appearance of gregariousness, is not a club man,

Dougie and Kate with Madiba. The Malletts have always had dogs in the family – Nick even took his dog Rumpus to France!

preferring the small group of family and close friends. He would rather play aggressive bridge – he is the best player in his bridge-playing family – with his sisters than be at a posh function. He might be away at weekends but home during the week to take children to school, play golf with Dougie, watch Kate's gymnastics and so on.

For Nick Mallett a holiday place is, as it had been in Du Toit's Kloof, somewhere like Rietvlei in the Kouebokkeveld where there is no electricity, just a huge dam and bass and waterfowl and gentle dragonflies perched like pennants on the tips of reeds and the only sound the pinging of plovers, the songs of the *kokkewiet*, the cries of ducks and the rounded vowels of frogs. Or Knysna, with its variety of activities and friends and family. Or at their house at Greyton (which they owned for 14 years till 1998), with its river at the bottom of the garden and the pool for bathing and the birds and the mountains all around and the unbroken peace. Nick and family have more joy out of being with the family than sampling sophistication.

For Jane, the problem of matches remains the unbearable tension. She has found them hard to watch, even on television, and spends most of the match walking round the swimming pool of their Constantia home, waiting for shouted updates from Dougie at the television set.

Before he took the job of Springbok coach, a job he desperately wanted, he and his family discussed the position a great deal before applying. After all, such an application would change their lives. It might even mean riding into horrific storms. It would open them all, parents and children, to the spotlight, which can at times be cruel, as the Markgraaff family knew only too well.

Nick went off to his daughter Kate's sports day at Herschel and was beaten by his brother David in the Fathers' Race. It made the press.

From the start of Mallett's appointment, the light of publicity was always there.

EDUCATION

The idea for the foundation of the Western Province Preparatory School (WPPS), known irreverently as Wet Pups, belongs to Sir Percy Fitzpatrick, one of South Africa's outstanding characters – businessman, miner, farmer, statesman, parliamentarian and author, whose most famous book is *Jock of the Bushveld*. In 1912 Fitzpatrick invited Christopher Stansbury of Oundle School in England to come to South Africa to found a private preparatory school in Claremont. Stansbury was succeeded by John Pridmore and then by his own son, John Stansbury, who was also for a while the headmaster of Springvale in Zimbabwe.

The school belonged to the Stansbury family and Mrs Stansbury felt constrained to sell it – there was the possibility of that it might be made into a hotel. Fortunately the Cape Town Old Andreans persuaded St Andrew's in Grahamstown to buy the school and raised the money in debentures to do so. On 1 July 1959 WPPS became the property of St Andrew's College, which sent down Ted Rivett-Carnac from St Andrew's Prep to run the school. He was the headmaster when Nick Mallett was at Western Province Preparatory School.

Nick bore boarding school stoically at the time. After all, his father's position required it, and this cohesive family always did what was best for the family. But he wanted to be a day boy and Anthony and Vivienne were not totally opposed to the change. Ted Rivett-Carnac persuaded them to leave him there – as a good example to others. He was, apparently, the only boy in the boarding house who would immediately own up if he had done something wrong!

Honesty has always been his strong suit and, at times, it has got him into trouble. He has said his say the way he has wanted to say it, often loudly, usually vigorously, backed up by a big presence and, especially when he was younger, with a cavalier lack of diplomacy. This has not always gone down well with rugby administrators who are even more untouchable than referees. But it was a distinct virtue in his dealings with his players.

On one occasion he was sent home from WPPS with chickenpox. When it was running to an end, Vivienne found that Nick was licking the scabs which had come off and sticking them back on in the knowledge that when the last one was gone he would have to go back to boarding school. It was his mother's first inkling that Nick did not really like boarding school and it hit her hard. But Nick was always able to shrug off difficulties as if they did not exist and get on with things. The same was true of people whom he did not get on with or looked down on. They ceased to exist and he got on with life.

Being only 4,2 kilometres from home, his parents would keep up with him and his activities, but he was still required to write home. Later, when he was at St Andrew's, he and his father would write to each other, by aerogrammes. His friends remembered that some letters came handwritten, some typed. The typed ones were usually about formal and unpleasant business. Nick would be in some trepidation if a typed letter came from home and would remain gloomy and withdrawn after one had arrived.

When they were at home, the invitation the brothers feared most was one from their father to play a game of snooker at Kelvin Grove. That was the time for a fatherly discussion of a corrective nature.

Vivienne felt a certain telepathy with Nick. On one occasion she was returning home, felt some strange premonition and turned the car around to go to WPPS where she found a destroyed Nicholas. He had been dropped from the rugby team and his world was in tatters.

At WPPS Nick played for two years in the 1st XI and the 1st XV and won the award for the most promising boxer in 1968. Swimming was very much a forte as well. In 1968 he won the Under 12 high jump at WPPS sports day while David won the Under 8. Nick ended his WPPS career by passing the entrance exam to St Andrew's, and with full colours for rugby, cricket, swimming, boxing and athletics.

He was also a choirboy and acted in *The Pirates of Penzance*. As a new boy at St Andrew's he also sang in the choir but somehow it did not suit the heaving

The Western Province Prep Cricket XI in 1968. Nick Mallett is third from the left in the middle row. Peter Golding is back left. The captain is Rupert Gull.

MALLETT FAMILY COLLECTION

sportsman. Play-acting remained a big activity, as it was with his parents. His first rôle had been as a shepherd in a nativity play when he was three – 'inclined to bash his lamb about somewhat', his mother recorded.

At Western Province Preparatory School Peter Dauncey, who succeeded Ted Rivett-Carnac as headmaster, took Nick for rugby. He had come to WPPS from Springvale and later moved to Highbury in former Natal where one of his pupils was Bobby Skinstad. Peter McPherson took Mallett for cricket and Peter Cronwright was the choirmaster. The choir, who sang at Bill Schroeder's wedding when he was a teacher at WPPS, spent the ceremony gazing in wonder at the bride. Nick was then ten years of age!

In 1969 he was sitting the St Andrew's scholarship exam when Miss Dorothy St Hill, a legend at WPPS, noticed that he was missing from the Maths paper, an exam which she was invigilating. She sent for him. He was found oiling his cricket bat with linseed oil and arrived at the exam, shirt soaked with oil, hands unsuited to mathematical neatness. There was, presumably, also some oil on the bat. In 1970 Nick went to St Andrew's College in Grahamstown.

ST ANDREW'S

St Andrew's College was founded in 1855 by John Armstrong, the first Anglican bishop of Grahamstown, then a frontier town but soon to be known as the City of Saints and Scholars because of its many churches and educational establishments, including Rhodes University. Run on English public school lines, St Andrew's mingles easily with the gracious town. It is largely a boarding school, with a strong house system, a school that believes in tradition. In the early 1970s the school had roughly 470 boys, which was regarded as the optimum number.

Getting to and from St Andrew's was a slow process in those days – a train journey of 36 hours through the Karoo, leaving at 9 pm on Tuesday to arrive on Thursday morning. Boys will be boys, and the twenty or thirty Cape Town fellows found ways of amusing themselves, which included consuming beverages such as beer and slipping rapidly to the pub in Alicedale.

When Nick Mallett came to St Andrew's, Canon John Aubrey was headmaster, but was not in good health. Roger Clark was acting head for a while and then Eric Norton took over in.1972 as the fourteenth headmaster. Norton was very much an Old Andrean. He was also a star sportsman in his day, playing cricket for South Africa and captaining the Junior Springboks at rugby.

Nick Mallett was a new boy when his parents went to Greece and England on long leave. About four days out from Cape Town on the voyage back, Vivienne had an uneasy premonition. When they docked, Anthony's mother, who had settled in Cape Town, was there to meet them with the news that David had mumps. That was obviously what the premonition had been. Vivienne felt relieved. But as they walked into the house, the phone was ringing. It was St Andrew's, to say that Nick had suffered a burst appendix and was not in good shape.

MALLETT FAMILY COLLECTION

St Andrew's Under 16A in 1972. Nick is second from the left in the front row.

She immediately flew to St Andrew's. Nick hugged his mother, crying and saying: 'The worst is you didn't even know.' The fifth change of medicine worked and Nick flew home with his mother to recuperate, 'looking like spaghetti', she said. Some of his convalescence was spent in the Ashton district on the farm of Paul de Wet, an old boy of Bishops with sons at the school at the time.

Mallett first made his name at cricket, at a time when Tony Greig, later to captain England, was the school's professional coach. When the St Andrew's Colts toured the Western Cape in 1971, Mallett took 5/42 in the victory over Wynberg and then 4/29 in the surprise victory over Bishops. At that time Anthony Mallett was coaching the Bishops Under 15 team, a good side.

The very first ball of the match struck Nick Pagden, the St Andrew's opener, on the pads and Anthony gave him out. The Pagdens and the Malletts were good friends and at that stage Vivienne Mallett was sitting with the Pagdens. It was a tense moment, and Buller Pagden got up and went for a diplomatic walk. Later Anthony did not give Nick out when he snicked the ball but his son saved the family honour by walking.

When Bishops batted the two Nicks, Pagden and Mallett, took five wickets each to win the match for St Andrew's.

The next year he was in the 1st XI and was invited to Nuffield Trials, where the Eastern Province team would be picked to attend Nuffield Week, as the provincial tournament for schools was then called, but he was not chosen). In 1972 he was

MALLETT FAMILY COLLECTION

Nick Mallett, centre-stage, in a tense moment as Proctor in *The Crucible*.

awarded cricket colours. Already he was described as a 'great competitor', as he dominated the school's bowling. In 1973 he toured the United Kingdom with the 1st XI, taking 8/46 against Radley, a famous public school at Abingdon near Oxford. One of St Andrew's successes on the tour was victory by 66 runs over Haileybury, when Mallett took 3/16. He took 20 wickets on the tour, far and away the best bowling for St Andrew's. When he went off with the Eastern Province Schools XI to the Nuffield Week in Bulawayo in 1973, Anthony flew up to watch his son.

Mallett was a niggardly bowler. Losing was worse than not winning, and one way to avoid losing and certainly to keep one's analysis within bounds was to bowl wide. Asked by his captain once what field he wanted for an aggressive batsman, he replied: 'It doesn't matter. I won't be bowling within reach.'

Playing in a social match on one occasion his side set their opponents 290 to win in just three hours. Mallett put four men on the boundary, bowled wide of the off-stump and had Tim Brukman on the boundary shout: 'Hit the ball! Make a game of it!'

His rugby progress was slower. In his Under 15 year he rebelled against playing lock. Despite his clumsiness and lack of speed, he wanted to play fullback, as his father had done. Mike Holderness, the Under 15 coach, agreed but told Mallett he would then have to play in the B team, which he did.

In his Under 16 year he started growing into the massive man he became, and he ended up playing lock – a reluctant lock. He was angry with Axel Ohlsson, the St Andrew's coach, for playing him there. Mallett did not get on with him or his housemaster, Alan Sanderson. They were authoritarian men in an authoritarian age, not men the rebellious headmaster's son easily related to. He was, as now, outspoken, which led to inevitable clashes.

On one occasion, Anthony, a great letter writer, wrote to Alan Sanderson:

> *'I am well aware that Nicky is aggressive of opinion and that this is not always tempered with dignity or tolerance. The latter he will learn; the former will, I hope, come with maturity.'*

The sportsfield was Nick Mallett's biggest outlet as a schoolboy. In 1973 he first played in the St Andrew's 1st XV rugby team and was awarded colours. In 1974 he was awarded colours for cricket, rugby and athletics. He was also the first St Andrew's boy after Dudley Gradwell in 1964 to play both Nuffield cricket and Craven Week rugby.

Sport certainly played a bigger part in Nick Mallett's school life than academics did. His mother wrote of him in 1971:

> *'Nicky, whose letters give ball-by-ball descriptions of cricket matches or, in winter, kick-by-ruck descriptions of Rugger, seems to be putting work rather low on his priority list but he scrambles through – all 6½" of him.'*

The stage continued to be important at St Andrew's. In 1970, remarkable as the thought may be, he played the part of Mrs Highness in AA Milne's *The Boy Comes Home*, and produced 'a little gem of acting', according to the review. Female parts were not easy to cast at an all-boys school! The next year he was in *The Dear Departed*, when the review said he had 'a tendency to growl inaudibly'.

Nick had two exceptional rôles in plays at St Andrew's. In 1973, in Barry England's *Conduct Unbecoming*, he played Major Alistair Wimbourne, VC, the macho, massively strong officer. On one evening, Wimbourne was talking to one of the rare females available to officers when the junior subalterns drew closer. With a flourish he said: 'Away with you, the whole pack of you.' And, suiting gesture to words, he flourished his sword, and, as would be likely to happen to Nick Mallett, the tip of the sword caught the end of Anthony Ball's nose. In the best traditions of the theatre, Ball, a Rhodes Scholar in 1983 and later a successful businessman, carried on despite the bleeding. He was playing the part of Boulton.

Conduct Unbecoming won the Lynette Alexander, the Border schools' drama trophy. In his review John Axe wrote: 'As Wimbourne V.C., N.V.H. Mallett, suitably blustering in manner and heroic in proportion, carried through the denouement with a convincing rough sympathy.'

The play in 1974, Arthur Miller's *The Crucible*, in which Mallett played Proctor – who was hanged in the Salem witch-hunt – was somewhat less successful. The review stated: 'N. Mallett's portrayal of this full-blooded character was undoubtedly the best single feature of a good production.'

SCHOOL REPORTS

In 1974 David joined Nick at St Andrew's. It was possibly not always easy having such a high-profile brother at the top of the school. David did not enjoy St Andrew's, but Nick's own relationship with the school was a pragmatic one. He was there and would get from the school what he wanted. He was never the classic leader at school and certainly not a conformist. His leadership was based on great talent and a forceful personality.

On one occasion, when he was a house prefect, he dropped off to sleep in his study and did not make chapel. Inevitably his absence was noted and he was sent up to Eric Norton, the headmaster.

Norton said to Mallett that he was like his horse and needed the correction of the crop. Mallett agreed that he was in need of discipline but thought that in his case the crop was unnecessary, as he tried to talk his way out of a hiding. Eric Norton disagreed. He demoted Nick, who was a prefect. Then he gave him 'six of the best', and again promoted him to prefect. After all, one did not beat a prefect.

Mallett walked away from the headmaster's study, past Chris Danziger, the history master whom Mallett respected greatly. Mallett, who was rubbing his backside in pain and anger, was due to baby-sit for the Danzigers that evening. He caught sight of Danziger, got his emotions under control and asked: 'When do you want us tonight, sir?'

'Six,' replied Danziger. And then he asked: 'Have you by any chance had a beating?'

'Six,' replied Mallett and rushed out, leapt over the railing, down a floor to the road and ran back to Armstrong to counteract the sting in his tail.

Baby-sitting for the Danzigers always meant an evening out of the boarding house and a mountain of ham sandwiches which Mrs Danziger would leave for the baby-sitter. On one occasion Chris Danziger had got only as far as the end of the road when he realised that he had forgotten the cinema tickets. He returned to find Mallett next to the kitchen table mildly embarrassed because the plate of sandwiches was empty.

Nick Mallett responded to the sporting challenge, usually in his own way, and to the academic challenge of somebody like Chris Danziger, who could cut through the detail to what was important, interesting and intellectually challenging. Apart from that Danziger was a good cricketer.

He enjoyed the less conventional masters – David Hogge, who produced *Conduct Unbecoming* and *The Crucible*, John Axe and Bob Sutherland – because they were widely read and for their sense of humour. His own sense of humour varied from the subtle to the practical joke which was occasionally crude.

In 1974 Pierre Moureaux, a Frenchman whom Mallett thought unusual, was doing post-matric at St Andrew's. He was busy with a chemistry assignment for the UNISA course (University of South Africa, the biggest external university in the world) he was taking and came back to his study for a cup of tea. Mallett locked him in, three storeys up. The Frenchman protested volubly but Mallett left him locked in. The protesting and the incarceration lasted three hours till Pierre was set free. In the meantime his experiment had exploded in a vast and useless mess.

HEADMASTER'S REPORT.

Nicholas is to be congratulated on the award of The Old Mutual Cup. He is a grand and exceptional fellow and probably realizes only too well that the only problem he really has is to direct just enough of his tremendous energy and zest into channels which will bring him more lasting benefits.

He was certainly one of the characters of his year and will go far if he controls himself. EBH P.T.O.

MALLETT FAMILY COLLECTION

Eric Norton reports on Nick in the Michaelmas term of 1974.

Nick did not always get on with his fellows who often found him arrogant. At WPPS he was frequently in fights though such occurrences were rare at the school. But Mallett was always true to himself. He did what he wanted to do and then was wholehearted.

On the other hand his ego, seemingly dismissive, was easily bruised by people for whom he had a high regard. Tim Brukman, one of Nick's closest friends, says that what he first liked about Mallett was his sensitivity.

The line between dismissive confidence and arrogance is a fine one. Bob Bolus, who played with and against Mallett for many years, said of him: 'Lots of people have thought Nick arrogant. But when you get under the skin, you find a wonderful, intelligent man.'

To Brukman, his next attractive quality was his enthusiasm. Any suggestion would be met with enthusiasm. At four on a freezing winter's morning, you could wake Nick and suggest a swim and he would be instantly awake and say: 'Hell, that's a great idea.'

Unbounded energy and determination, with the ability to make tough decisions and a massive physical presence, would seem to add up to a tough guy. In many ways he is physically and mentally tough, but he is also the tough man who cries in the cinema. His children make him cry, and tough decisions keep him awake at night. Brukman was right about sensitivity.

School reports do not always reveal this side of Nick but tell a fairly succinct story of his whirlwind approach to school life.

The Marandellas School of Equitation
RIDING REPORT, 1963
Nicky is always cheerful and willing 'to have a go', full of energy and enterprise but finds it difficult to co-ordinate his hand and leg movement.

He appears much more secure on a horse now than at the beginning of the year, though I think he stays on more by luck, balance and practice than good judgement, as he rarely appears to have the correct part of the anatomy in contact with the saddle! He also undergoes constant trouble with his clothes.

Springvale
EASTER, 1963
Nicholas joins in all school activities with great energy and enthusiasm. If he were rather less untidy and absent minded, he would make life easier for himself.
BD JOHNSON – HOUSEMASTER

Western Province Preparatory School
JUNE, 1964
A very honest little boy.
W THOMAS – FORM TEACHER

DECEMBER, 1968
An outstanding year in play, a satisfactory year in work, an erratic year in behaviour. An adult appreciation of what is important will turn him into an outstanding character.
TED RIVETT-CARNAC

St Andrew's College
MICHAELMAS, 1970
On the whole Nicky has had a very good first year and promises to become a force in the land.
TERRY STEVENS, HOUSEMASTER IN MALLETT'S FIRST YEAR AT ST ANDREW'S

EASTER, 1972
For Nick everything is much larger than life and he finds it difficult to exert the sort of self-discipline that would enable him to cope with the mundane and sometimes petty things of life.
ALAN SANDERSON– HOUSEMASTER

EASTER, 1972
It can be said of Nicky that he does not know his own strength. His strength of limb is undoubted, as seen in all sports and in the way he breaks things 'it just came apart in me 'ands, Mum'. He has strength of character that he has not yet put to full use. His mental strength is beginning to develop. I am looking forward to being around when all this latent potential is realised.
ALAN SANDERSON

EASTER TERM, 1974
Nick is a great competitor on the games side and can also be somewhat exuberant. He can also be very impetuous and I do hope that he will not embarrass his team and his coach this rugby season. He is such a fine player but must learn control.
ERIC NORTON

MICHAELMAS, 1974
There is almost a deathly hush about the place, so much life has left Armstrong since Nick's departure.
ALAN SANDERSON

[At the end of 1998, Dougie, Nick's nine-year-old son, received a report which read: 'He works with great enjoyment and enthusiasm but he still needs to learn to temper his boisterous nature.' Which suggests familial traits!]

A report of a different kind appeared in the annual report of the Cape Piscatorial Society in 1970:
'The climax came on 28 December 1969 when the Liesbeek yielded the biggest rainbow of the fishing season, apart from one taken many miles away at Ceres. Two junior members, aged 13 years, Nicholas Mallett and Michael Bing, went to the Wall Pool and were lucky to find a celebrated inhabitant in a careless mood. Nicholas cast a brown fly and a big fish came at it, and it seems that one of its rushes brought it right to the bank where they stood. Without ceremony, Nicholas and Michael took to the water and their combined efforts resulted in the fish and the boys finishing the contest above the water line, high if not dry.

'It was a beautiful coloured and conditioned female rainbow of 21½ inches, weighing 5 lb. 2 oz., C.F. 52, weighed and measured in the club room. (Illustrated in PISCATOR No. 77). It was truly a record for the Liesbeek.'

The whimsy of the report was not matched by the anger of the Piscatorial Society members at having such a prized rainbow trout so impetuously caught!
[The Liesbeek is a river, more stream than river especially in the dry summer season, which wanders down from Table Mountain and on through Newlands and Rondebosch towards Table Bay.]

At the end of 1973, Mallett matriculated with a university entrance pass. The result was first given in error as a School Leaving Certificate. Naturally, this caused much consternation in the family home. Finding the error was great relief. It was a good enough result to get him into the University of Cape Town (UCT).

For all his so-called lack of achievements academically, Mallett never failed a single exam and his last, at Oxford, went well indeed.

UNIVERSITY

It is obvious from all who taught him and knew/know him, that he, with his obvious intelligence and energy, was an underachiever on the academic front. His schoolmates at St Andrew's say that he never did any work. His post-matric year was spent at the pool, reading a book (he remains well read) or practising diving, and then getting ready for the afternoon's sport, to be followed by bridge in the evening. There were always sweet girls at UCT, and his mother to take notes for him and get him through exams.

At UCT, too, was Chris Danziger, who moved there from St Andrew's in 1975. He lectured Mallett in history and in the education faculty. Danziger moved to Oxford and Mallett arrived there nine months later. When Mallett was at Saint-Claude the Danzigers visited regularly. Danziger said of Mallett: 'He was certainly a very successful pupil, not only for his cricket and rugby, but my recollection of him is also as a very able historian.'

He finished his BA at UCT in 1977 with majors in history and English. In 1978 he received his Higher Diploma of Education, equipped to be a teacher. His teacher training during 1978 was, not surprisingly, at Bishops. He actually taught for six months – at Fairmont in the Cape Town suburb of Durbanville in 1983, an experience which he thoroughly enjoyed, but he was a stand-in as there was no permanent post available. Besides, he realised that on a teacher's pay he was likely to battle financially and could not see himself ever owning even a house. When he came back to South Africa after living in France for nine years, he again wanted to teach and applied to his dad's old school, Bishops, for a post, which unfortunately he did not get.

Mallett was a graduate student at University College (Univ), Oxford, from October 1979 to June 1981, when Lord Goodman, the Labour Party lawyer who was made a life peer by Harold Wilson, was Master, and came down with an upper second for the diploma in Social Studies. The studies did not start all that promisingly for his tutor flung back his first essay, telling him not to waste his time. That sort of challenge ensured that Mallett's studies went well.

Life at Oxford was not all sport. His studies prospered, social life was active and he found time for bridge. He and a friend, Paul Kumleben, decided that they would like to represent Univ in the inter-college bridge championship, called Cuppers, but their suggested entry caused mirth in the college. They then entered as a non-representative pairs team and did far better than the official Univ team, winning seven or eight rounds and reaching the semi-final of the university bridge competition. He did not, as has regularly been said, win a Blue for bridge, if for no other reason than that there is no such thing, though the Oxford University Bridge Club would like to have Blues.

In his Under 20 days for Western Province it was not long before he had a bridge school going with players like Gareth Jones, Stephen Joffe and Steve Hofmeyr. Efforts to teach massive Flippie van der Merwe were not successful even though Mallett started simply enough with rummy. On Springbok tours there were always card games. On the 1996 tour to Lille many of the players went to a disco after the match against the French students, and there was Mallett in an alcove with several players, playing cards.

'JOBS'

Apart from teaching, his 'jobs' included some time at BP and Westex. He joined BP when he came back from Oxford, the first job he had ever had. First he was placed in their office for financial planning and realised that figures were not really his métier. He was moved to marketing where he spent some nine months visiting petrol stations. BP mapped out his future, how they saw his promotions and his transfers, but Mallett did not see such a future and went to play rugby in Italy instead.

While at BP, he was playing golf at Royal Cape when, to his horror, he saw the managing director, Ian Sims, also playing golf. Nick Mallett unceremoniously flung himself into a ditch and the frightening moment passed. It went without comment, but Sims dined out many times on the story!

He was with Westex for some two years, a job which suited him as it set him free to concentrate on rugby. A parent of a boy at Fairmont, Wessel Hepburn, offered him a position in marketing with his firm which was seeking to expand in the casual clothing market. They tripled his schoolmasterly pay and gave him a car and job which was not 20 per cent as demanding as teaching. That he was playing for Villagers at the time, along with Piet Geldenhuys of Westex, was not a drawback when it came to getting the job!

His working career has mainly been rugby oriented. The bistro in Saint-Claude was really about rugby. He has dabbled in tourism, but it was mainly about organising French rugby teams touring South Africa.

Rugby has been a sport, passion and job to Nick Mallett, and it has not let him down. Mallett himself believes that he has been incredibly lucky. He has been doing what he loves doing since 1985 and gets paid to do it. And for all the pressures that go with it, he has found the job of Springbok coach wonderful.

South African Schools team in France, 1974. Nick is standing sixth from the left.

PLAYING CAREER

Nick Mallett's rugby career really took off in 1974, while he was still at St Andrew's. Before that he had excelled at cricket, having been on a tour to England with the St Andrew's cricket team and to the Nuffield Week in Bulawayo, the same Nuffield Week attended by Allan Lamb and Peter Kirsten, both of whom went to great fame at cricket.

He was in post-matric at St Andrew's but not yet 18 when he was chosen as a lock for the Eastern Province rugby side to play at the eleventh Craven Week in July 1974. Nick was elected the vice-captain of Eastern Province (EP) Schools. They played a pre-Craven Week match against Border, whose star was Ian Greig, the brother of Tony Greig who captained England at cricket. Before the match the EP players formed a huddle to say a prayer. The vice-captain, perhaps because he was from a church school, thought this was a poor idea. EP lost to Border 16-12 that day and there were suggestions that the vice-captain's heathenism was the cause. He never came to terms with praying before rugby matches and would possibly consider himself an agnostic.

It was not a particularly good Craven Week for Eastern Province who were thumped 36-6 by Orange Free State but managed to beat North Eastern Cape and Far North.

Nick Mallett was invited to the SA Schools rugby trials held in East London from 28-30 September 1974, where an SA Schools team would be selected to tour Italy and France. Dr Danie Craven, the president of the SA Rugby Board, did not like the idea of using Craven Week, which was meant to be a festival, as trials, and so separate trials were held to choose the team for Europe.

After the muddy trials, manager Jan Preuyt, who had been a Dutch Reformed missionary in Nigeria and was a man of remarkably conservative views, presented his team to the president of the SA Rugby Board for his approval, normally a procedure of rubber-stamping. Craven looked at the team and sent Preuyt back to his selectors – 'to think again'. They presented their team to Craven the second time round, who again sent them back. The third time they arrived the good doctor approved, for on this occasion Nick Mallett, whom Preuyt considered fractious, was in the team. Craven had recognised Mallett's worth. When later Mallett was chosen to play for South Africa, Craven recalled his selection for SA Schools and said to Mallett: 'There is always one who comes through. You are one of them.'

THE TOURING TEAM WAS: Dawie du Toit, Gerhardt Weitz, Bob Bolus, Shane Carty, Mark Cawood, Agie Koch, Lallie van der Linden, Wim Hancke, Bruce White, Rob Hankinson, Mark Kleinenberg, John Matthysen, Nick Mallett, George Rautenbach, JP Geldenhuys, Mark Thompson, Warren Kruger, Fanie Campher, Lee Barnard, Ernst Kruger, Ockert Stoop, John Bonthuys, Mike Laubscher, Daan Roux and Bernard Pienaar (captain).

It was a team of particularly fine schoolboy players.

Nick Mallett is the only one of that team who played for South Africa. Notable players at Craven Week that year who did not make the SA Schools team were Flippie van der Merwe, André Markgraaff, Willie du Plessis and David Smith.

As was typical for South African rugby teams abroad at that time, the SA Schools tour was beset by political problems. In Italy the uncertainty made the players downhearted; for the management it was an ongoing headache. Italian rugby in the 1970s was nothing like what it was to become in the 1990s and it was subject to pressure from world abhorrence of apartheid.

In Italy, sport, including rugby, fell under the banner of the national Olympic committee (CONI), and that committee disapproved of contact with South Africa. But although this was the first South African team to tour in Italy, there were several South Africans playing there at the time – Des Newton, John van der Spuy, Nelson Babrow, Tjokkie van der Merwe, Tommy du Plessis, Donovan Neale-May and Gertjie Nortjé. These players played against the schoolboys who in all nine matches on the tour played against senior players. And Amos du Plooy, the former Springbok prop from the

The Eastern Province Craven Week team in 1974. Nick Mallett, who was the vice-captain and playing at lock, is second from the left in the front row.

Eastern Province, was there, helping Italian rugby along and helping with the tour's organisation. And he refereed all five of the matches the team played in Italy!

The police were instructed to guard all rugby fields in Rome to prevent the South African schoolboys from playing on them. Rugby fields under arrest! But the players went off to a soccer field at a school and played against the Dick Greenwood XV.

From Rome they went up into the cold of the Alban Hills to play against another selection side and then down south to sunny Reggio-di-Calabria. They were to have played against the University of Naples, but the home side was forbidden to play by the Italian Rugby Federation. Instead they got a match against a team called Italsider. The fifth match was against the University of Genoa. Nick Mallett, not surprisingly, played in all five matches. He was not a man who would take omission easily! And besides, captain Bernard Pienaar had been unavailable after hurting his neck in the sea at Clifton Beach when the team was preparing for departure. Mallett missed the sixth match in Nice but played the seventh, at Maubourguet, some 25 kilometres from Tarbes in the south-west of France. He did not play in the last two matches.

The boys played nine matches, winning them all, scoring 444 points while conceding only 61.

And how did the fractious young player get on?

The touring party was split along language lines. The Afrikaans-speaking players conformed, the English speakers, especially Mallett, did not.

On Christmas Eve in Paris, the English speakers, led by Nick Mallett and Lee Barnard, decided to see what the city was like. They did not get back till between 11 and midnight, only to find the management waiting up for them. Preuyt threatened to send them home.

Remorse did not fill Mallett, who simply did not toe any line. Preuyt said afterwards that Mallett was talkative but no trouble whatsoever and Stoney Steenkamp, the team's coach, had no problem with Mallett's behaviour, apart from his talking. *'Hy het my mal gepraat.'* (He talked me into insanity). From his point of view Mallett practised and played well.

In Paris Steenkamp and Preuyt took it in turns to stay in the hotel to keep an eye on the boys. Preuyt went for a walk and 'accidentally' ended in Place Pigalle with its interesting ladies. As he was wandering back he saw a figure duck behind a car. Curious, he went behind the car which sent Mallett, and others, fleeing down the road, coat tails flapping.

One afternoon in Tarbes the team went up into the Pyrénées to ski. Jan Preuyt came down on a toboggan, which went out of control. To stop it he turned it over, bruising his upper arm. Back at the hotel Preuyt and some others, including Mallett, went into the heated pool in the hotel. Tracksuits were removed and in they went. The players got out leaving their manager behind, still exercising his bruised arm.

Inevitably, when Preuyt emerged from the pool, his tracksuit was gone. He waited in hope but help did not come, and that evening they were due to entertain the South African ambassador. Eventually, peering carefully around corners, Preuyt ventured out. The coast was clear. He made it to the lift. The lift was empty. He reached his floor. The corridor was empty. Gratefully he sprinted down the corridor to his room. As he went, laughter gathered from the rooms, Nick Mallett's most obvious of all.

When the team returned to South Africa, some thought the tour a waste of time, but Danie Craven was at the airport to welcome them with pride. He said: 'Big joke my foot! Our schoolboys did a wonderful job for us in Europe.'

Nick was nominated as one of the Eastern Province sports stars of 1973. The other rugby nominees were Hannes Marais, the Springbok captain, and Gavin Cowley, whose omission from the Springbok team that year remains a mystery to most.

In 1975 Nick Mallett went to the University of Cape Town (UCT), a coup for the rugby club there, which did not receive nearly as many Craven Week players as rivals Stellenbosch, let alone SA Schools players. His days as a lock forward were over; from now on he played number 8 or flank.

UCT

Dr Craven had been right – the boy had potential. In his first year at the University of Cape Town, not yet 19, he played for UCT Under 20, SA Universities Under 20, Western Province Under 20 and UCT 1st XV. And he played first league cricket! After all, cricket was really the game at which he first excelled.

In his first year at UCT he went with the cricket team to the South African Universities' Tournament in Durban, an occasion of some cricket and much undergraduate jollity. During the stay, the UCT team went to the beachfront amusement park and Mallett and some team-mates went through the Chamber of Horrors. As each ghost or skeleton came frighteningly out of the darkness, Mallett rose and punched it, till he eventually capsized his vehicle and short-circuited the whole Chamber of Horrors, causing the UCT team to flee in disarray before the owner.

For one cricket season, just before he left for France, he played for Techs club in the Cape and was the chief wicket-taker in first league cricket in the Western Province. There were, however, also two incidents in which umpires stopped umpiring because of him. On one occasion he was sitting apart in a black mood during the tea break. One of the umpires came and sat next to him, remarking that he was clearly unhappy with some decisions and asking him what the matter was. It was a silly question. Mallett told him, and the umpire left the ground.

The next week he was bowling against Western Province Cricket Club in a match in which there was only one umpire, who walked from one end of the field to the other. Mallett got a wicket and in came his close friend Nick Pagden. Pagden missed the first ball, which was followed by a verbal barrage from Mallett. Pagden slashed at the second and was dropped in the slips, which increased the barrage. The third hit him on the pads and there was a loud appeal for LBW, which the umpire turned down, causing raucous chagrin. The next ball, the last of the over, was, as Pagden expected, a bouncer. Pagden hooked it out of the ground into the swimming pool, which occasioned much anger, including an altercation with the umpire, who then walked off home.

MALLETT FAMILY COLLECTION

Returning home after the 1974 South African Schools tour. On the left is Bob Bolus and his mother Lucia, then Nick Mallett and his father Anthony and sister Jenny.

At one stage in Western Province club cricket, bonus points were given for batting and bowling. Every two wickets the fielding side received a bowling bonus point. Mallett was playing for UCT when Eddie Barlow, one of South Africa's greatest and most competitive cricketers, came in to bat. From square leg came the Mallett voice: 'OK, chaps. Here comes a walking bonus point.'

The UCT Under 20 rugby side in 1975 was remarkably successful. It beat a magnificent Stellenbosch team when Stephen Joffe scored a thrilling try, and won the Under 20 league. The next year Nick Mallett was playing in the UCT first team under Cecil Moss, a coach ahead of his time and for whom Nick had high regard as a strategist, a whole-hearted coach. Tim Hamilton-Smith, the Varsity Under 20 coach, brought Mallett and Peter Munnik from the UCT first team for the Under 20 match against Stellenbosch as a curtainraiser at Newlands for the Hedley Atkins Shield. Mallett broke an ankle early in the match, and UCT were thrashed as they had never been thrashed before! Stellenbosch scored over 70 points.

The ankle was pinned and put in plaster. Wearing a plaster cast on his ankle was an enormous restriction for Mallett and he destroyed it three times before they changed the cast from plaster of Paris to fibreglass, Dr Jerome Sedgwick's solution to his impatient patient's destructive energy.

Nick Mallett's first match for Western Province Under 20 was in 1975, a victory of 34-12 over Eastern Province. The report read: 'The big rangy flanker, Nick Mallett, had an outstanding game, goaling three tries, two of which were from the touch-line and booting over a long-range penalty.'

Mallett, as always, went about developing his career in a rebellious fashion, but his sheer talent kept his progress racing along. When there were high jinks in a hotel, which sometimes included the removal of hotel furniture via a window, Mallett would

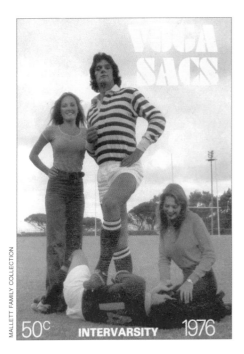

UCT's brochure for Intervarsity 1976.

be in the thick of it, often aided and abetted by his old WPPS mate, Mark Hampshire. And he was seldom quiet. Mallett said what he wanted to.

UCT were to play Stellenbosch at the Coetzenberg stadium that year when Dave Williams, their kicker, was injured and unable to play. UCT did not have a kicker. And so they brought Mallett into the side. Tim Brukman was at flyhalf, but he did not tackle. His team-mates knew that but Mallett did not.

During the match a Stellenbosch centre broke past his man. Brukman covering could have got him but declined to do so. Mallett covered like a fury but was not quick enough to make the saving tackle. Stellenbosch scored.

Nick Mallett came storming over to Tim Brukman and gave him a rude piece of his mind. Brukman, who barely knew Mallett at the time, replied: 'I don't tackle. Secondly, it's not your place to tell me what to do. Thirdly, you're in this team to kick, not talk.' They became the firmest of friends.

In 1976, only 19 years old, Mallett was chosen for Western Province B when they lost 36-28 to Transvaal B in what used to be a traditional friendly at Newlands. He was outstanding at No. 8.

Then came one of the big matches of his career. Danie Craven always regarded Intervarsities as test matches – the test of character, ability and nerve. There are several contests between universities in South Africa but the main Intervarsity is that between Cape Town and Stellenbosch. The first time Newlands ever had a crowd of 30 000 was for the Intervarsity, with its ceremonies and singsongs and student high jinks.

The University of Cape Town are called Ikeys, Stellenbosch Maties. The names were originally pejorative nicknames. Cape Town students called the Stellenbosch students Maties from their habit of calling one another *maat* or *matie* (chum or chummie). The Maties then thought up a name for UCT and called them Ikeys because there were many Jews at Cape Town University at the time (1918). The UCT Student Representative Council objected and arranged to meet their Stellenbosch counterparts one Friday afternoon. But it turned out that there were no trains to Stellenbosch on a Friday afternoon, the meeting did not happen and both nicknames became names of honour used by each university.

The contest between the two universities had been level pegging till the 1950s, after which Stellenbosch started to pull away. In the 1960s Cape Town won only once, in 1961, and there were no Intervarsities in 1973, 1974 and 1975 due to political wrangling. The UCT principal, Sir Richard Luyt, wanted all races to participate but the government refused. But in 1976, the Minister of Sport, Piet Koornhof, agreed to an open Intervarsity.

In the rain, UCT, spearheaded by Nick Mallett, gained a famous victory – 10-3, a goal and a try to a late penalty goal, though the Maties were hot favourites. Stellenbosch had seven players who either were or became Springboks. Ikeys were captained by Chris Pope on the wing and had Peter Whipp at centre.

The try that made the match came off Mallett – a move called Lochore, after Brian Lochore, the All Black captain who used it in 1970. The move depended on a slow heel at a firm scrum on the left-hand side of the field. Mallett detached from the scrum, just behind the last feet in the scrum and some 5 metres to the right of the scrum. The flyhalf moved out to the right and so did the inside centre, both about 10 metres back from Mallett. It looked like a decoy move. Or possibly the flyhalf or the centre could cut back and take a scissors pass from Mallett.

Dave Zietsman, the UCT scrumhalf, passed to Mallett who was facing the scrum. The UCT centre cut back for the expected scissors pass. Mallett turned toward him and kept turning and instead fed Tim Brukman who was coming straight and at speed on the outside. Brukman went through without a hand laid on him.

> Cape Town team: Dave Williams, Alan Cunard, Dirk Hoffman, Peter Whipp, Chris Pope (captain), Tim Brukman, Dave Zietsman, Doug Mather, Pete Ingwersen, Doug Claxton, Giles White, Jack Gibberd, Butch Deuchar, Rob Wagner, Nick Mallett.

> Stellenbosch team: Dawie Snyman, Bossie Clarke, Gerry Catherine, Christo Nel, Leon Oosthuizen, Robbie Blair, Divan Serfontein (captain), Paul Salkinder, Sean Povey, Piet le Roux, Jan Boland Coetzee, Schalk Burger, Hennie Bekker, Hein du Toit, Henry Muller.

It was young Nick Mallett's Intervarsity, the match that 'revived Intervarsity' as it once more became competitive.

Afterwards Nick was walking back with Tim Brukman to Kelvin Grove, the famous old sports club across the railway line from the Newlands stadium, when he suddenly saw his father, who spotted his son at the same time. The two rushed together and leapt into a massive embrace.

But father and son did not always see eye to eye when it came to performances on the field. When Bishops beat St Andrew's at Bishops in a match where the surreptitious Bishops tactic – which worked – was to upset Mallett's temper and thus reduce his effectiveness, Anthony expressed sympathy with his son who told him, in direct, staccato and not necessarily educated tones, to go away.

PROVINCE AND MORE

In 1976, too, Mallett played for Western Province Under 20 when they lathered Western Transvaal 46-8, and then he was the surprise choice for the Springbok trials on 21, 23, and 26 June in Pretoria, with a final trial in Durban on 6 July. After all, the old foe was at the door: Andy Leslie's All Blacks started their tour of South Africa on 30 June 1976 in East London.

When Mallett was chosen, statisticians went diving for their records to find a younger forward to be invited to Springbok trials. They found other young trialists – DO Williams, Johnny Bester and Freddie Turner – all teenagers but all backs. A teenage forward at Springbok trials was unprecedented.

And he got his first bit of fan mail – a letter from Miss Brenda Fabian of Fish Hoek, who asked for an autographed photograph.

AC Parker, the great rugby writer of his time, spoke of Mallett's aggressive, intelligent play. He was regarded as one of the finds of the trials, but then, two years before, Dr Craven had passed his verdict: 'This boy is outstanding. He is a footballer to his fingertips.' And the doctor was not a man given to praise, believing that it could make a man self-satisfied and destroy him. The 'boy' at the time stood 1,94 m (6 ft 4 ins) tall and weighed 97,5 kg (215 lbs), and there was fire in his belly.

Six teams took part on the first day of trials – Combined Services, SA Country, Currie Cup A, Currie Cup B, SA University A and SA University B.

In those days the 22 provincial teams were divided into three groups – Currie Cup A, Currie Cup B and Sport Pienaar. The Services (armed forces and police) had a good side and the universities were powerful.

Nick Mallett on the charge against Orange Free State in 1976. The other players are, from the left, Wouter Hugo, Jan Boland Coetzee, Theuns Stofberg and Piet du Plessis.

On the second day of trials, the trialists were divided into six teams on merit. Nick Mallett, 19 years of age, was at No. 8 in the B team, opposing Wynand Claassen. Claassen would succeed Morné du Plessis, the Springbok captain, who had missed the trials through injury. In that trial, the A Team beat the B Team 22-21. But that did not help Nick, as he was dropped to the C Team and did not make the final trial in Durban at all.

VS THE ALL BLACKS

A Gazelles team (SA Under 24) was chosen to play the All Blacks in Port Elizabeth on 20 July 1976. The match was played on the Tuesday before the first test in Durban, which the All Blacks subsequently lost. It was sandwiched between two All Black defeats, for on the previous Saturday, in a thrilling game, Western Province came from behind to beat the All Blacks by a Robbie Blair conversion from touch. After the defeat by Western Province at Newlands, the All Blacks suffered a loss of morale going into the first test. Six of the players who played in Saturday's test had also played against the Gazelles – Bryan Williams, Duncan Robertson, Tane Norton, who captained the team against the Gazelles, Kent Lambert, Hamish Macdonald and Peter Whiting. The first five had also played against Western Province. It was a tough week for the All Blacks. The Gazelles match was no bagatelle.

> GAZELLES: Doc Louw, Cheeky Watson, Christo Wagenaar, Dirk Froneman, Hermanus Potgieter, De Wet Ras, Barry Wolmarans, Noel van Rensburg, Wouter Hugo (captain), Ockie Oosthuizen, Corrie Pypers, Eben Jansen, Hennie Bekker, Theuns Stofberg, Nick Mallett.

The Gazelles led 15-9 with ten minutes to go. Then New Zealand's Bryan Williams got round Cheeky Watson for the equalising try. With three minutes to go, All Black Duncan Robertson missed a drop goal attempt, the ball bounced away from Doc Louw in in-goal and Joe Morgan scored the winning try. The New Zealanders won 21-15, scoring three tries to one, but De Wet Ras kicked 11 points. Sir Terry McLean, New Zealand's greatest rugby writer, thought the Gazelles 'wretchedly unlucky'. He picked out the best of the Gazelles and said that 'a boy, who was thought to be a Springbok in the making, Nick Mallett, certainly showed promise at Number 8, though there was a suspicion that he had been praised too much'.

In his report on the match Neil Cameron said: 'In the tight loose Bekker, Stofberg, Pypers and Mallett did well for the Gazelles, standing their ground and making their opponents fight for every ball.' One could not imagine Mallett playing rugby, or any game for that matter, in any other way.

He was then chosen for the Quagga-Barbarians to play the All Blacks but withdrew because of his broken ankle. It was a sad match to have missed, a real thriller, which the All Blacks won 32-31. At one stage in the second half the Quagga-Barbarians led 31-9 but the All Blacks scored their winner on the stroke of time.

The 1976 Gazelles. Mallett is second from the left in the back row.

At the end of 1976 the SA Rugby Writers chose five players of the year and five promising players of the year. The five players of the year were Morné du Plessis and Moaner van Heerden of South Africa, and Sid Going, Bryan Williams and Pole Whiting of New Zealand – three All Blacks although they had lost the 1976 series against the Springboks. And Bryan Williams was chosen the Player of the Year.

The five promising players of the year were Dirk Froneman, Wouter Hugo, LM Rossouw, Divan Serfontein, whose first match for Western Province was against the All Blacks, and Nick Mallett.

1976 was a very good year for Nick Mallett's rugby career.

1977

In 1977 Nick Mallett was a leading light in the UCT first team. When they beat Northerns 33-6 to start the season, Johan Gerber wrote: 'The Ikeys were confused, bewildered and baffled until Nick Mallett, their lanky Gazelle No. 8, decided to take matters in hand.'

Match reports were not always complimentary or indeed consistent. When UCT lost its next match to Bellville, Neville Leck of the *Cape Times* reported: 'With massive delusions of grandeur, Mallett tried abortively to take on the entire Bellville team.' AC Parker of *The Argus* wrote on the same match: 'Nick Mallett was a tower of strength at No. 8 for UCT, spearheading many a drive.' The glories of the 1976 Intervarsity had evaporated, and in 1977 Maties clobbered the Ikeys 48-9.

On 11 July 1977 Nick Mallett was on the flank for a South African Invitation XV against a Rhodesian Invitation XV at the Police Ground in Salisbury (now Harare). The eighth man was Tommy Bedford. His immediate opponent was Fergus Slattery who was playing for the Rhodesian XV. Both sides scored six tries but the South African team won 33-32.

The Springboks would play a test in 1977. Loftus Versfeld was celebrating a revamped stadium, referred to as the new Loftus Versfeld at the time, and a World XV would come to South Africa. In the third week of July three days of trials were held in Pretoria – racially mixed trials, for the very first time in South Africa's history. It is astonishing in retrospect, but, in 1977, it was regarded as a massive breakthrough.

On the final day of the trials, Mallett was placed in the D team along with Timothy Nkonki, Bridgman Sonto and Turkey Shields. The D team beat the C team 22-12.

At the trials a Gazelles team was chosen to play against SA Country Districts. The Gazelles, managed by Dougie Dyers, included Chris Rogers, Divan Serfontein, Eben Jansen, Gerrie Sonnekus (captain), Henning van Aswegen and Nick Mallett – all destined to be Springboks – and Gavin Cowley, who should have been one. More remarkable was that players not classified as white were selected for SA Country: Timothy Nkonki, Turkey Shields and Errol Tobias, while Hennie Shields played for the Gazelles. The Gazelles won 28-24.

That year Mallett was on the flank in the place of the injured Jan Boland Coetzee in a Western Province team which played against Northern Transvaal at Loftus Versfeld, one of the most controversial matches in South Africa's rugby history.

There were 65 000 spectators at Loftus Versfeld, a record gate for a Currie Cup match. Western Province were leading 13-12 when Morné du Plessis, the captain of Western Province, tackled Naas Botha, who was 19 years of age and already the darling of Loftus.

The referee penalised Du Plessis, a debatable decision, Botha was taken off on a stretcher, Pierre Edwards goaled the penalty to give victory to the Blue Bulls, and Morné du Plessis was escorted from the field by a protective guard of policemen.

Just after the Pretoria controversy, Doug Hopwood, one of South Africa's all-time greats and the best No. 8 in the world in his time, said of Nick Mallett: 'One of the stars of the "new" Western Province pack is the tall, alive, forceful Nick Mallett. To my mind he has potentially everything that's needed to be a great rugby player. My personal view is that, if the selectors want to make the pack more efficient, they should move Morné to flank and boldly put Mallett at No. 8.'

Charismatic Morné du Plessis did not relinquish the No. 8 position until his retirement in 1981. He was the Springbok No. 8 and captain.

Before the 1977 test Western Province played against the World XV at Newlands and gave them a whopping hiding – 56-26, 11 tries to five – in a match in which Mallett's display was described as fiery and magnificently aggressive. Mallett ended 1977 playing for a Coastal XV against an Inland XV in Durban, as part of the Glenwood Old Boys' Sports Expo '77 festival organised by Rodney Gould, the former Springbok fullback. The Inland team won 43-40.

1978

Mallett started 1978 in grand fashion hitting the winning runs for UCT off Peter Swart in a thrilling cricket match. In March he went on the UCT rugby tour to Rhodesia. At Intervarsity that year, Stellenbosch seemed to hold all the trump cards but it took a late try by Bob Bolus and a conversion by Robbie Blair to give them a 15-13 victory before a crowd of 27 000. Nick, described as 'enormously virile and aggressive', scored one of UCT's two tries.

His performance was enough to cause a bombshell in the Western Province camp. The selectors dropped Jan Boland Coetzee, flanker, Springbok and Western Province icon, the most capped Western Province player of all time, in favour of Mallett. The great man played instead for Western Province B against Boland B, which many people thought a needless humiliation but which Coetzee accepted with his usual uncompromising determination.

Mallett kept his place in the Western Province side for the Northern Transvaal match in Pretoria. Again, it was a match to stir the blood, with the final result 19-all.

In 1978, UCT beat Rand Afrikaans University (RAU) 31-22 but were thrashed 44-6 by Stellenbosch. After this a combined Southern Universities side was chosen. The practice of doing this had a long and glorious history in the Western Province, dating back to 1886.

The team was chosen to play against the United States Cougars, who were touring South Africa. There were only two Ikeys in it – Peter Munnik at centre and Nick Mallett on the flank while Rob Louw from Stellenbosch was at No. 8.

> TEAM: Hannes Pretorius, Bossie Clarke, Christo Nel, Peter Munnik, Pierre Goosen, Robbie Blair, Martyn van Blommestein, Bill Nieuwoudt, Sean Povey, Hempies du Toit, Tollie Oosthuizen, Piet du Plessis, Bernard Pienaar, Nick Mallett, Rob Louw.

The match, played on a sodden, muddy Newlands field, was won 16-7 by the Southern Universities.

At the end of 1978 the SA Rugby writers chose ten players in each position. They placed Mallett sixth amongst Number 8s, after Morné du Plessis (Western Province), Gerrie Sonnekus (Orange Free State), Thys Burger (Northern Transvaal), Chris Oosthuisen (Griquas), and Menanteau Serfontein (Eastern Province). The previous year he had been fifth – after Morné du Plessis, Wynand Claassen, Gerrie Sonnekus and Alan Sutherland, the All Black who was playing for Rhodesia.

ENGLAND

It was a fairly quiet year, 1978, and at the end of it Nick Mallett went to London en route for Oxford. At the same time Morné du Plessis, then Peter Whipp's business partner, asked Peter's sister Jane if she would like to be a nanny in Chelsea as friends of his were looking for one: Jane McKenzie, a South African girl, had gone with her Canadian husband to live in England, and so off Jane Whipp went to their home overlooking the Royal Chelsea Hospital.

While waiting the nine months to go up to University College at Oxford, Nick worked at the Sun Inn in Richmond and played for Richmond, the classy South London Club founded in 1861.

Nick Mallett made his début for Richmond against London Scottish on 3 March 1979. He also played in their drawn club championship match with Gloucester, which permitted Gloucester to advance to the next round on the strength of being the visiting side. It was not a good season for Richmond but the Incredible Hulk, as they called him, made a great impression. David Rollitt, the veteran England loose forward still playing for Richmond, had this to say: 'The boy has everything. His potential is as great as any loose forward I have played with or against. In our present state England cannot afford to ignore him. He's a really mean version of Andy Ripley. Andy Ripley is an athlete playing rugby. Nick is such an abrasively competitive ball player that when the thunder cracks I know I am going to be all right. Playing alongside him has given an old man like me a new lease of life.'

In April 1979 Nick was chosen to tour South Africa with Middlesex. In Cape Town on 12 May he played against Western Province, a match which the home side won 29-15. Included in the Middlesex side were Chris Ralston, Tony Boddy, Andy Ripley, Terry Morrison, Graham Birkett, Alan Lawson, Mark Taylor of New Zealand and Kevin Bowring, who had played for Wales B, became a schoolmaster and coached Wales in the 1990s. When the Springboks played Wales in Cardiff in 1996, Kevin Bowring was their gracious coach. But he could not survive Wales's litany of defeats.

OXFORD

From Richmond Mallett went up to Oxford to University College, called Univ, Oxford's oldest college, founded in the middle of the 13th century. Mallett worked as a barman, studied and played cricket and rugby as well as many other games. At Oxford he was awarded a Blue for cricket. In a match against Glamorgan he scored 50 runs and took five wickets – his fifty included three sixes off Ian Botham.

Jane went to Oxford with him and worked as a waitress. Although they were still going out, she later returned to South Africa to finish her degree.

In Oxford the big rugby occasion was the Varsity Match, played at Twickenham on the second Tuesday of December each year. The tradition of the match goes back to 1872. As with all traditional matches there are many ceremonies before and afterwards and because students are involved, they are usually great fun.

On 1 November, in the lead-up to the Varisty Match, there was the annual quiz between the Blues team and the Oxford Referees' Society. The quiz was drawn 40-all. The report in *Blueprint*, the Oxford publication at the time of the Varsity Match, said: 'The hospitality of the referees was tremendous, as usual. Mallett was as happy as a sandboy, arguing for hours on end with any referee he could get to listen.' (In all of Mallett's career as a player and a coach, referees have tended to be the enemy!)

Nick Mallett has never been at a loss for words. The report on the quiz states: 'His captain insists that he would win, not so much a Blue, as a Purple Heart for talking.'

Plenty of serious rugby was played before the Varsity Match. In 1979, Oxford played 13 matches, winning six and losing the rest. Their record was much better than Cambridge's and included victories over Richmond and Blackheath.

One of the matches – the Stanley's match – was a long-standing Oxford tradition, first played in 1919. Robert Vinen Stanley, born in 1872, died in 1957 and known to people as Uncle, never went to Oxford and probably never played rugby football. But from 1910 to 1923 he was the Oxford representative on the Rugby Football Union and was an England selector for two seasons, 1913-14 and 1921-22. He started the Greyhounds (the Oxford 2nd XV) and just after World War I introduced the match between the Blues and Major Stanley's XV.

In 1979 Oxford lost 7-6 to Major Stanley's. The match became a bit stagnant, less and less supported by the public. Then, in the mid-1980s, Derek Wyatt, the former Blue and England player, got involved, brought in Yamaichi as a sponsor and overseas stars, and restored the match to its former status as a major fixture.

Mallett had a good Stanley's match in 1979 when he shut out Terry Holmes, the powerful Welsh scrumhalf, and another good game when Oxford played Trinity College from Dublin and Mallett got the better of Donal Lenihan, the Irish No. 8 (who was the Irish manager in 1998). The England selectors were watching and were impressed.

In 1986, when he was in France, Nick Mallett had the honour of captaining Major Stanley's XV. Mallett scored a try in his team's 26-18 victory. In his team were Jean-Baptiste Lafond of France, Simon Halliday and Rory Underwood of England, David Sole of Scotland, Michael Lynagh of Australia and Neil MacDonald, the South African who had captained Oxford to victory in 1985.

THE VARSITY MATCH

The Varsity Match is a grand social occasion, with the arrival in the West Stand carpark of charabancs, cars with open boots, food hampers and lubricants! For a while, interest in the game had dwindled, but in 1976 Bowring, the insurance company, got involved, then overseas players were introduced and soon Twickenham was full again for the Varsity Match.

The match itself, on 11 December 1979, was seldom a spectacle or of a high standard but Oxford duly won. It was a drab match and condemned as such. To be fair the windy, blustery conditions did not help. The headline to John Mason's article read: 'OXFORD'S MALLETT TIPS SCALES IN RAGBAG GAME.'

John Mason, one of the best rugby writers, wrote: 'Oxford having said beforehand that they could scrummage all day, proved the point tenfold at Twickenham yesterday. But in taking the Bowring Bowl from Cambridge they will not have won many new friends.

'Victory in the 98th University match by a dropped goal and two penalty goals to a penalty goal will have pleased only those devoted to the Oxford cause. Enterprise was a rare commodity.

'Mallett, the No. 8, played with an unfettered enthusiasm and involvement that mark him as a player of immense potential. There is a fury about him that makes the result of his current match the most important thing in the world.

'His colleagues recognise this sufficiently that once Roberts, the lock, clapped a restraining hand over Mallett's mouth. The No. 8 was not at all pleased with the decision of the Cambridge touch judge – and said so.

'Oxford were leading 6-3 just before half-time.

'The points that meant that Cambridge needed to score twice for victory came immediately before half-time. Already they are probably part of the Mallett legend. With only his second kick of the season in a match, he put the ball over from 45 yards.

'Mallett, known to his colleagues as the White Hunter, should have left it at that, because later he was way off target. But if Cambridge do not release the ball in similar circumstances next year, I suspect that Mallett, probably as captain, will be equally successful.'

The touch judge, who occasioned an emotional outburst from Nick Mallett and a restraining hand from lock Nigel Roberts, was John Robbie, who had captained Cambridge to a famous victory the year before when he scored 17 of Cambridge's 25 points. It is the custom of the Varsity Match that the previous year's captains, in blazers, run the line as touch judges, even though they might have only the vaguest of knowledge of the Laws of the Game.

Oxford had a rolling maul moving towards the Cambridge line. Mallett was controlling the ball at the back of the maul and some 3 metres in from touch as the maul veered infield and Mallett plunged over for a try which Allan Hosie, the well-known international referee from Scotland, awarded.

But there was John Robbie in his light blue blazer and carnation standing with his flag up. He claimed that the Oxford maul had been in touch. Hosie cancelled the try and awarded the line-out. Mallett hurled the ball at Robbie and told him that he was a cheat. Robbie, who was trying to maintain some sort of dignity in front of the vast audience, says that he told Mallett to back off or he would ram the flag into a painful place, but says that he said it softly.

Immediately afterwards Robbie spoke to Hosie and discovered that he had been wrong. The line-out should not have been ordered as the edge of the maul had touched the touch-line, not the ball or the ball-carrier. Robbie went straight to the Oxford changeroom to apologise. Mallett admired that ever after.

Peter West of the *Sunday Times* wrote: 'As an exercise in the frenetic activity anticipated at Twickenham on the second Tuesday in December, yesterday's University match no doubt had something to commend it. But in other respects it fell so sadly short of expectation as to be rated one of the poorest matches in the series that one can recall.'

He described Mallett's kick as follows: 'Mallett thumped home a penalty goal from just inside the Cambridge half.' The kick was about 8 metres inside the Cambridge half and straight in front of the posts.

Wilfred Wooller, who died in March 1997, was a great all-rounder. In the 1930s he won Blues for rugby and cricket, played rugby and squash for Wales and was centre-forward for Cardiff City. He said of the 1980 Varsity Match: 'I did not think it possible for the educated mind to descend to such a subterranean low performance. It was a kicking disaster of the magnitude that defies description.'

The negative criticism of the match worried Mallett not a jot, for Oxford had won and he had kicked a penalty goal. After all, Oxford backs were poor and Cambridge had good backs. The fact that Marcus Rose had chosen to kick continuously, thereby playing into Oxford hands, was not Oxford's fault.

Nick Mallett had carried out his main duty of the day – nullifying Paul Ackford in the line-out.

THE OXFORD TEAM WAS: TME Davis (Hale School, Western Australia and Baliol); EAK Quist-Arkton (Taunton and St Benet's Hall); SJ Halliday (Downside and St Benet's Hall); AC Thomas (Colston's and Keble); DK Woodrow (Queen Elizabeth Grammar School, Wakefield & Regent's Park); RB Clark (Brinkburn Comprehensive and Christ Church); DJ Morgan (Bablake and Keble); TW Jones (Mill Hill and Wadham); SM Hofmeyr (Diocesan College and University); TP Enevoldson (RGS Newcastle and Brasenose – captain); KJ Budge (Rossall and University); NT Roberts (Glenalmond and Jesus); WEA Morrison (Felsted and Oriel); CN Bray (Leeds and Keble); NVH Mallett (St Andrew's and University)

The win put Oxford 43-42 ahead of Cambridge in the series of matches, played since 1872. Cambridge had never headed Oxford in the series. They did so for the first time in 1981 when they beat Oxford in thick snow.

On the night following the match there was Vincent's Twickenham Ball at the Café Royal in Regent Street. Tickets for the dance only were £15, for the dinner and the dance £25. The function would run from 8:30 pm to 2:30 am.

Mallett remembers the function as a student binge which ended when some students emerged singing *Heigh-ho, it's off to work we go* and dropped their trousers, which ended as a photograph in the *Sunday Times* supplement.

As is the custom he was then appointed captain of Oxford for the next year. In fact he did not play the Varsity Match that year because of injury, and, unusually, Peter Enevoldson captained Oxford for the second successive year. Enevoldson was remarkable, for he played in five Varsity Matches. It was usual for players in the Varsity Match to be limited to four appearances.

BARBARIANS

Two days after Christmas Mallett, was invited to play for the Barbarians against Leicester, a singular honour. The Barbarians, a club without property, whose members are elected, was founded in Bradford in 1890. The club's motto, devised by WJ Carey, who toured South Africa in 1896 and returned later as the Anglican Bishop of Bloemfontein, is 'Rugby football is a game for gentlemen in all classes but never for a bad sportsman in any class.'

THE BARBARIANS: KM Bushell (Harlequins), J Carleton (Orrell & England), NJ Preston (Richmond & England), R Bertranne (Bagnères & France), MAC Slemen (Liverpool & England), WG Davies (Cardiff & Wales), SM Lewis (Ebbw Vale), M Burnett (Heriot's FP), M Luke (St John's Pirates & Canada), IG Milne (Heriot's & Scotland), WB Beaumont (Fylde & England), JP Scott (Cardiff), J-P Rives (Toulouse & France), CW Ralston (Richmond & England), NVH Mallett (Oxford).

On a slushy field in driving rain at Leicester, the Barbarians slogged out a 9-8 victory.

CLOSE TO ENGLAND

The All Blacks were on tour in October 1979. Nick Mallett was chosen as a reserve for the London Division, as London Counties had come to be known, who just lost to the All Blacks 21-18. He was part of the England squad for the test, which New Zealand won, drably, 10-9. His rôle in the England squad had really been as 'cannon fodder', providing contact at practices.

He was also chosen to play flank for the Rest against England at Twickenham on 5 January 1980, a trial match. There was the possibility of an England cap as the Lions were to tour South Africa that year under the captaincy of Billy Beaumont, who was also the England captain.

Mallett himself said: 'If I can get any kind of chance at an England cap, I will snap at it. I am English by birth.' In later years, as the successful Springbok coach, there was hardly ever an article in the English press on Mallett or quoting Mallett which did not refer to his English birth. He did not play in Gilbert & Sullivan's *HMS Pinafore* but it was still, to the English press, 'greatly to his credit, that he is an Englishman!'

England beat the Rest 28-10. Gerry Parsons of Bath replaced Mallett at half-time as a trial substitute. The England flanks in the trial were Mike Rafter and Roger Uttley. Also in the Rest team was Nigel Horton whose place Mallett would one day take in France.

Mallett was captaining Oxford late in 1980 when they beat Richmond and London Scottish and then, in October that year, against Northampton, disaster struck. He tore the medial ligaments in his knee and missed rugby, starting again only in 1982.

Huw Davies, the Cambridge captain, also missed the Varsity Match through injury. Mallett wrote him a letter of commiseration. He had an operation, wrote his exams in May and went home to South Africa on holiday.

The injury gave him more time for cricket, for which, like his father, he was awarded a Blue. He also played for the combined Oxford and Cambridge side. André Odendaal, at Cambridge at the time, was also in the team. He remembers that he and Mallett were far more competitive about their cricket than the other Oxbridge players, who seemed to regard cricket as a 'Sunday afternoon at Uitsig'. Mallett was especially tough and was the dominating personality in the dressing room.

CURRIE CUP

Nick Mallett was back in the Western Province in 1982, an auspicious year. It was the centenary year of the oldest rugby union in South Africa and, no matter what others may say and no matter what their results may be, the most prestigious. It has always been the arbiter of good taste in South African rugby, and in the Western Province, the spirit of the game runs deep. The spectator support has been the most constant and, at least in its own view, knowledgeable. Most Springboks have come from the Western Province, and Western Province has won the Currie Cup most frequently.

The Currie Cup, named after Sir Donald Currie, the owner of the Union-Castle Line, has always been South Africa's premier rugby competition. In the period of South Africa's absence from international rugby, the Currie Cup became the Holy Grail of South African rugby, producing the highest of rugby passion.

For Western Province, there had been a Currie Cup drought since 1966, when it had last won the tournament, then organised on a league basis. From 1968 Currie Cup finals became annual events of enormous passion, the life-blood of the South African Rugby Board as the chill grip of isolation grew tighter. But between 1968 and 1981 Western Province played in only four finals. There was the shared final in 1979, but no victory besides. In the 20 finals between 1939 and 1981, Western Province had won only in 1947 and 1954. Yet it remained the province with the greatest aura of prestige.

Then came 1982. Jan Pickard was elected the president of the Western Province Rugby Football Union on 24 February 1981, in succession to Hannes Pretorius who had died of a sudden heart attack on 12 January 1981. Pickard had been a trustee of the Union but had not played any other part besides being intensely interested. From the time of his election Western Province became his passion. As a successful businessman, success on the rugby field was of paramount importance. In business, success equalled profit; on the rugby field it equalled victory. In South Africa that meant the Currie Cup.

In 1981 Western Province performed poorly – in that season they won only six of eleven Currie Cup matches, scoring only 19 tries. This was not acceptable to Jan Pickard who had a fairly cavalier attitude to rugby's amateur principle.

In 1982, in a most effective move, the great Theuns Stofberg transferred from Pretoria to Cape Town, not only to develop his practice as a physiotherapist but also to play for Western Province. He was the great forward of his age, playing flank or lock, a giant of a man with speed, intelligence and skill. De Villiers Visser, a Western Province man but playing for Defence in Pretoria, came home. Hennie Bekker, that most Province of Province men, finished his military training in Bloemfontein and returned to the Cape. The competitive, skilful prop Henning van Aswegen came from the then Orange Free State. There were also others like Hempies du Toit and Shaun Povey. Amongst the backs were the three Du Plessis brothers – Willie, Michael and Carel – and players of the calibre of Calla Scholtz, Colin Beck and Niel Burger. Michael du Plessis, an erratic talent of great proportions, brought a refreshing unpredictability to the fly-half berth. And big Nick Mallett replaced Morné du Plessis, who had retired.

Western Province had always been noted for its creative back play. 'Give us 40% of the ball and we'll win', they used to say. For the next five years their success would rest squarely on the massive backs of their pack of forwards and a large proportion of possession.

Mallett's performance against Northern Transvaal at Newlands in 1982 was possibly the greatest of his life and a turning point in Western Province's fortunes.

Northern Transvaal were a powerful lot, but Western Province took them on at forward, Moaner van Heerden, Louis Moolman, Jannie Breedt and all. The men who made it work were Paul Lombard, the friendly, strong Van der Stel scrumhalf, and Nick Mallett at No. 8. Lombard picked up and played to Mallett, who drove. It was a drab theory that thrilled the Newlands crowd with its efficiency and effectiveness. Western Province won 24-13. To many it was Mallett's finest match. It would have an echo four years later when he and Francois Bonthuys adopted the same tactics and contrived to beat the 'Springboks' on their unhappy internal tour, which replaced, partly and unsatisfactorily, the cancelled All Black tour.

CHAMPIONS

Western Province just lost to Northern Transvaal away but there were no fears when the 1982 Currie Cup final was played at Newlands later in the season. Western Province thrashed the Currie Cup champions, Northern Transvaal (who were without Naas Botha), 24-7, three tries to one.

THE WESTERN PROVINCE TEAM: Colin Beck, Carel du Plessis, John Villet, Willie du Plessis, Niel Burger, Michael du Plessis, Divan Serfontein (captain), Henning van Aswegen, Shaun Povey, Willouw van Niekerk, Rob Louw, Hennie Bekker, Div Visser, Theuns Stofberg and Nick Mallett.

THE NORTHERN TRANSVAAL: Pierre Edwards, Cliffie Brown, Darius Botha, Dirk Hoffman, Deon Coetzee, Giepie Nel, Tommy du Plessis, Jan Oberholzer (captain), Willie Kahts, Piet Kruger, Burger Geldenhuys, Moaner van Heerden, Louis Moolman, Jannie Breedt, Johan Marais.

Of the Western Province team only Niel Burger and Willouw van Niekerk, whose career was cut short by a neck injury, did not play for South Africa. Brown, Hoffman, Coetzee, Nel and Oberholzer of Northern Transvaal did not become Springboks.

Theuns Stofberg remembered Nick Mallett in his playing days as the greatest self-motivator of the lot. If he scored a try or set one up for a team-mate, he would say in loud triumph: 'Well done, Mallett' or 'Mallett, you bloody beauty.'

He never stayed down for long, either. When, early in his career, the selectors dropped him from the Western Province side, he said to Tim Brukman: 'The selectors are mad. I mean, look at the way I'm playing.'

On one occasion he was playing cricket for UCT against Paarl, who were then in the Western Province first division. He started a new over to a new batsman, David Turner, an English professional playing for Paarl. Turner hit a screaming cover drive for four off the first ball and Mallett told him it was a lucky shot. He told Turner the same thing for each of the next five fours off the next five balls and at the end of the over, gave him a succinct but belligerent explanation of how lucky he had been to score a four off each of the six balls of the over.

His confidence meant that he was able to bounce back quickly. Lose to England at Twickenham, be depressed but pick the players up with gentle and positive talk and then recover completely.

Western Province won again for the next four years – no other team has ever won five successive Currie Cup finals. Nick Mallett was in the team in 1983 when they won 9-3 against Northern Transvaal in Pretoria, three kicks to one, before 65 000 spectators, while Naas Botha was away as a gridiron kicker for the Dallas Cowboys. Northern Transvaal had never lost a Currie Cup final at Loftus Versfeld before. Mallett was one of five Province players who played in all 17 Western Province matches that year, the others being Divan Serfontein, Shaun Povey, André Markgraaff and Rob Louw.

THE 1983 WESTERN PROVINCE TEAM IN THE CURRIE CUP FINAL: Calla Scholtz, Carel du Plessis, John Villet, Wilfred Cupido, Bertie de Wet, Johan Durr, Divan Serfontein (captain), Henning van Aswegen, Shaun Povey, Hempies du Toit, Rob Louw, Hennie Bekker, André Markgraaff, Theuns Stofberg, Nick Mallett.

Mallett was in the team again in 1984 when Western Province beat Natal 19-9 in the Currie Cup final and Orange Free State in the final of the Lion Cup, a knockout trophy. Both finals were at Newlands. It was the first time Western Province had won the Lion Cup, which was competed for from 1983 to 1994.

THE 1984 WESTERN PROVINCE TEAMS: CURRIE CUP FINAL: Calla Scholtz, Bertie de Wet, Goggie van Heerden, Carel du Plessis, Niel Burger, Michael du Plessis, Divan Serfontein (captain), Bill Nieuwoudt, Shaun Povey, Attie Strauss, Rob Louw, Hennie Bekker, Schalk Burger, Kulu Ferreira, Nick Mallett.

THE LION CUP FINAL: Calla Scholtz, Carel du Plessis, Faffa Knoetze, John Villet, Neil Burger, Michael du Plessis, Divan Serfontein (captain), Bill Nieuwoudt, Shaun Povey, Attie Strauss, Theuns Stofberg, Niel Hugo, Schalk Burger, Rob Louw, Nick Mallett.

Enjoying Currie Cup triumph in 1983. Western Province team-mates Nick Mallett and Rob Louw look on as Wilfred Cupido drinks from the cup.

In 1985 Mallett damaged the cruciate ligaments in his knee, playing for Villagers against Stellenbosch. He needed a month off but there were vital matches against Orange Free State and Transvaal to be played. At the time he was being challenged for his Province spot by Gert Smal and young Schalk Burger, and he also was due to go to France to play. There seemed no point in battling against injury.

Mallett said much later: 'When I was playing, winning the Currie Cup was a big thing for me. The Springbok jersey was something I yearned for but also knew there would be few opportunities to realise.'

In 1998, when there were multitudinous opportunities to win a Springbok jersey, James Dalton would say that every player's dream was to play in a Currie Cup final. A dozen or more tests were played each year but only one Currie Cup final. The Currie Cup remains the Holy Grail of South African rugby.

SPRINGBOK

In 1984 Nick Mallett, a Villager member at the time, played for South Africa. England came on tour that year to play two tests against the Springboks. Before the tests, trials were held in Port Elizabeth on 21 May 1984. The eighth men were Gerrie Sonnekus of Orange Free State and Boelie Serfontein of Eastern Province. Mallett was not there due to injury.

The injury was not a pleasant one. Big Flippie van der Merwe, who weighed 132 kilograms, had been successfully sued for punching a player but was back for Orange Free State against Western Province. Free State peeled around the front of a line-out. Mallett tackled and turned, ending up on top of a Free Stater. Along came Flippie van der Merwe and stood on Mallett's head. The wound to Mallett's ear required 25 stitches. Van der Merwe apologised immediately afterwards, claiming that it was an accident but film evidence would suggest that it was not.

A lawyer contacted Mallett and offered to sue. In those days of 'cowboys don't cry', it was not really done to cite or sue, so Mallett let it be. But he missed the Springbok trials for which he had been chosen for the A Team with Gerrie Sonnekus in the B Team. Consequently Sonnekus played against England.

In both tests, in Port Elizabeth and Johannesburg, the Springboks thrashed the visitors, winning 33-15 (three tries to nil) and 35-9 (six tries to nil).

Nick Mallett went on to play for Western Province against England, a match drawn 15-all, though England scored two tries to nil. It was a very poor performance by Western Province.

Springbok determination as Mallett charges at Jaguar Xavier Miguens, 1984.

JAGUARS

The Jaguars were a South African creation, the brainchild of Dr Craven, to break South Africa's rugby isolation. Argentina would not, for political reasons, tour on their own to South Africa, but they could come as a South American conglomeration, chosen from Argentina, Uruguay, Chile, Paraguay, Brazil and Peru – but mainly Argentina. They were called the Jaguars and all their apparel, equipment, and even gifts, were supplied by South Africa.

They came first in 1980 before the Lions' tour and lost both tests to the Springboks, and were in South Africa again in 1982.

When they came in 1984 they had broadened their scope and brought two Spanish players with them. They were a more competitive side than England had been, with players like Diego Cuesta-Silva, young Fernando Turnes, Martin Sansot, Marcelo Campo, Fernando Morel, Diego Cash, Serafin Dengra, Gustavo Milano, Ernesto Ure, Tomas Petersen and, above all, Hugo Porta.

In October Springbok trials were held to select the team to play against the Jaguars. This time Mallett played in the trials, held at Loftus Versfeld. The eighth men were Gerrie Sonnekus (A team) and Mallett (B team). In the trials, the A team beat the B team 34-16 but there were three subsequent changes to the A team: Anton Barnard was chosen ahead of Hempies du Toit, Louis Moolman in place of Schalk Burger and Nick Mallett in place of Sonnekus. Mallett was apparently preferred to Sonnekus with a view to having a more robust player for the All Blacks tour the following year.

The Springboks beat the Jaguars 32-15 at Loftus Versfeld – Mallett's first test. From a sloppy line-out near the Jaguar goal-line, Nick Mallett plunged over and scored his test try. South Africa won by five tries to two.

Afterwards Mallett was capped by Danie Craven, who said to him with a grin as he capped his player: 'Right school, wrong university.' (Danie Craven had a soft spot for St Andrew's where he had taught.)

AN ABRUPT FAREWELL

In 1985 the All Blacks were due to tour South Africa and both countries relished the prospect of rugby's greatest rivalry. It was a massive blow to the All Blacks and Springboks when at the last minute, on a court order, the tour had to be abandoned because of South Africa's apartheid policy.

Trials, in which Mallett played, had already been held at Newlands and Stellenbosch in anticipation of the tour. So instead of playing the All Blacks, the Springboks went on an internal tour to play against 'Barbarian' teams, an unhappy tour that saw the local teams supported against the Springboks, especially at Newlands.

A team of 24 Springbok players was chosen for the tour. The loose-forwards were Burger Geldenhuys, Theuns Stofberg, Gert Smal and Gerrie Sonnekus. No Mallett. Smal, who played flank against the New Zealand Cavaliers in 1986 and was clearly a better flank than eighth man, was Mallett's opponent when the Springboks met the Cape Barbarians. The Springboks beat the Transvaal Barbarians 36-19 at Ellis Park and then came to face the Cape Barbarians at Newlands.

The Cape Barbarians, captained by André Markgraaff, practised at Hamiltons, where Mallett, Markgraaff and Michael du Plessis plotted the downfall of the Springboks. The plan hinged on driving forwards where Francois Bonthuys would play through Mallett to the forwards. It worked. To the delight of the Newlands crowd of 20 000, the Cape Barbarians won 18-13.

The match ended with Mallett on the half-way line on the Grand Stand side of the field – just in front of where Daan Swiegers and the other selectors were sitting. He looked up at them and stabbed a gesture of defiance in their direction. It was the end of his playing career in South Africa – to all intents and purposes. His family were embarrassed by the gesture which would continue to be recalled throughout Mallett's career. Nick Mallett said later, many years later: 'I'm not proud of it.'

THE CAPE BARBARIANS: André Stoop, China Bell, Danie van der Merwe, Michael du Plessis, Niel Burger, Giepie van Zyl, Francois Bonthuys, Frans Erasmus, Shaun Povey, Hempies du Toit, Schalk Burger (jnr), Hennie Bekker, André Markgraaff, Andrew Alexander, Nick Mallett.

THE 'SPRINGBOKS': Calla Scholtz, Carel du Plessis, Danie Gerber, Faffa Knoetze, Ray Mordt, Naas Botha, John Robbie, Henning van Aswegen, Wessel Lightfoot, Flip van der Merwe, Rob Louw, Louis Moolman, Schalk Burger, Theuns Stofberg (captain), Gert Smal.

The Springboks went on to beat the Central Barbarians and the SA Barbarians, for whom Mallett did not get a game.

In 1985 Western Province beat Northern Transvaal convincingly to retain the Currie Cup and won it again the next year when they beat Transvaal. Mallett played in neither final.

He was injured in 1985, and by 1986 he was in France.

FRANCE

At the end of 1985 Mallett went to France. The man behind his move was Dugald Macdonald, the most creative of No. 8s who had also played for UCT, Western Province and South Africa. Dugald was playing for Toulouse at the time, forming a wonderful loose trio with Jean-Claude Skrela and Jean-Pierre Rives. Nigel Horton, the combative English lock, had played for Toulouse before going to Saint-Claude as player/coach and manager of the village's bistro. Horton was leaving Saint-Claude and the club wanted a replacement of stature. Horton spoke to Macdonald, who had been a contemporary of Peter Whipp at Bishops and afterwards, and Macdonald phoned Mallett.

Nick and Jane were not long married and keen to travel. South African rugby seemed in a cul-de-sac with no prospect of good international competition; the players were getting tired of playing the same opposition three or four times a year to keep the coffers filled.

Off the young Malletts went to Saint-Claude in the Jura Mountains, only some 50 kilometres north-west of Geneva where the main sport is cross-country skiing, a cold part of the world in winter when rugby matches on thick snow were not uncommon. Nick had a three-year contract, but he stayed for five years. Their home was an apartment on the third floor above the bistro in the village square. The bistro was small and basic – a bar and ordinary tables and chrome chairs on a linoleum floor – but it became immensely popular, the rugby club's club house. Nick ran it remarkably well.

Some of his sales techniques were rather unorthodox. The village men would gather at the bistro after work, and they worshipped huge Nick Mallett, twice their size, to them a colossus. Mallett would go across to a man in the bistro who he thought was not drinking enough, pick him up by his shirt front and tell him to drink some more. 'Of course, Monsieur Mallett, for you I drink.' And he would put him down again amidst much good humour.

The locals loved drinking at Café le Club, especially after a home victory. Chris Danziger describes them: 'The rugby enthusiasts adored him, buying themselves endless unwanted drinks just for the sake of being around him, pressing bundles of notes on him, to which Nick returned some perfunctory and irrelevant change.'

In 1986 he had his 30th birthday in Saint-Claude, starting with touch rugby on the club's field. Thereafter the whole of the club descended on the small bistro for a sit-down supper. Soon rugby broke out and sets of forwards were scrumming against each other. Golf was being played with bottles of water for golf balls till the bistro was awash. And then the mob trooped off to a night-club called Le Bogart. It was a Nick Mallett evening.

Pete Golding and his wife visited and thought the apartment a hovel – up wooden stairs to three small rooms on the third floor. Vivienne Mallett thought it awful with its tiny sitting room, minute bedroom and cupboard for Kate, their baby, to live in! Furthermore, its toilet facilities were of a rural French kind – remote, uncomfortable and odorous. Jane thought the apartment quaint, a typically old French building, perched above the river. She remembered it as a cosy, happy time and eventually the third room became their children's room. And there was also space for the huge dog called Rumpus, which scarcely ever left Nick's side, not even in one of Saint-Claude's smarter restaurants.

Rumpus, who came with the Malletts from South Africa, was a remarkable dog. Nick would issue it with a command: 'Be a good dog' and Rumpus would go out to do his business, even if it meant going out into the Saint-Claude snow. Sometimes he would return and Nick would go outside and examine the evidence to find that the dog had cheated. Out he would go again, sometimes peeping round a bush in the hope that he could sneak back.

Life was not all rugby. Mallett probably played the best bridge of his life in Saint-Claude, playing two to three hours a day. He also played tennis on the slow clay courts and there was boule, the distinctively French game. Later Nick and his brother Dave joined up to become the Saint-Claude boule champions, more by aggression and intimidation of opponents than by genuine skill.

There was also golf at Divonne, east of Saint-Claude and tucked against the Swiss border. On one occasion Mallett teamed up with a stranger and went round chatting in French, only to find out afterwards that they were both English-speaking.

His golf was vigorous but erratic. Chris Danziger's son Martin played with him once at Divonne. When his father asked how it had gone, he replied.

'The first nine was very difficult,' he replied.

'And after that?' his father asked.

'We had to come in,' the son replied. 'Nick lost nine balls on the first seven holes, and we ran out of balls.'

People in France are passionate about rugby, which can be a good and a bad thing. It was good that tiny Saint-Claude, with a population of 13 000, had its own supporters' club and could produce crowds of 5 000 for every home match. It was tremendous that a club like Saint-Claude could end up in the French first league. It was great that Mallett's bistro became the social centre of the town, whose popularity depended partially on home victory.

It was not so good that the rugby, in sophisticated France, had a dishonest side to it.

Home teams won, and referees would find it hard to escape after a home defeat. If the referee had come up the mountain to Saint-Claude, he was in real danger trying to negotiate his way down, should he have been reckless enough to allow Saint-Claude to be defeated.

One year Saint-Claude reached the top of the Second Division and it was getting towards the knock-out competition. Mallett was on three yellow cards for ungentlemanly behaviour. Four would carry a two-match suspension. He wanted to get a fourth card early enough to be suspended before the knock-outs started, which would enable him to start with a clean sheet.

The opponents, Annecy, arrived and they had an ugly lock. In their previous encounter the lock had had plaster of Paris on one wrist. He covered it with a soft bandage and using his plastered wrist as a baton, went around bashing the men from Saint-Claude, breaking the hooker's jaw.

Mallett thought that this was a worthwhile way to get a yellow card. He moved himself from No. 8 to lock and, increasingly ostentatiously, punched the opposing lock at scrum time. The lock, away from home this time, did not react. Nor did the referee or the touch judges. It was after all a steep drive home.

Eventually Mallett could take it no longer. He marched to the front of a line-out and in full view of the referee head-butted the lock. The referee screwed his courage to the sticking point and gave Mallett, player/coach of Saint-Claude, a yellow card. Mallett thanked the referee profusely and left the field.

On another occasion Saint-Claude lost at home. The referee, aware of the dangers of the situation, did his best. He dished out penalties. He advanced them 10 metres and further. But he could not kick the ball over for them. Eventually, when Saint-Claude missed yet another sitter he blew the final whistle. People emerged from the crowd and made for the referee, who had to be escorted from the field. Later that evening, as he was negotiating his way down the Alps, an angry Saint-Claudian forced his car off the road, fortunately without damaging the referee.

The player/coach position meant that the demands on Mallett were that much greater. As a player, he had to do what he told them to do as a coach. He says: 'I learnt in France that you can say to a player only what you yourself can do.' It also meant that he had to give the lead when it came to fitness. The habit has not left him. 'I use running as a cathartic release from tension.'

When he coached Boland he was as fit as any player. As the Springbok coach he makes sure that he is in good shape. At the age of 42 he is lean, strong and fit – looking good enough to be playing.

A bonus during Nick's stay was the arrival of his brother Dave and his wife Karen. Dave Mallett had captained UCT and Villagers and played on the flank for Western Province B. He took over from Nick as player/coach/bistro manager after Nick's departure for Paris.

The only time the two brothers played together was in Saint-Claude, an experience which they enjoyed. It also brought them closer together. Dave scored many tries when Nick went on dummy runs, creating openings for his brother. But Nick was the one who did the hard work. He was the biggest in the team and so took the kick-offs and jumped in the line-outs.

Dave's life was not always easy at Saint-Claude. Nick ran the bistro but Dave at one stage had to be satisfied with a job changing tyres.

Dave had two matches in the second team and then Nick chose him for the first team. Their first match was a derby match away against Montchanin, a mining town in Burgundy close to Le Creusot, south-west of Dijon. The team, which included some Polish miners, was noted for its violent play, but Saint-Claude themselves were no angels.

The Malletts, not giants by South African standards, were taller than their opponents, and Dave reigned supreme at the back of line-outs. Saint-Claude was in the lead and this angered the home side. Dave felt very relaxed, but Nick heard the home coach shouting volubly to his players. Surprisingly, Montchanin threw to the back of the line-out where Dave caught and fed to his brother coming round on a peel. As Nick went to ground in a tackle he saw the Montchanin pack descending on Dave.

'Stay on your feet!' Nick shouted to Dave as he himself leapt up.

The two brothers stood back to back and the other Saint-Claudians rallied round. For more than two minutes battle raged. The Mallett brothers became a respected force in French rugby.

Eventually the match proceeded. Three players from Saint-Claude and two from Montchanin were sent off. A third home player left the scene for hospital as

Robert Natalie, the Saint-Claude prop, charged at him, using his head to shatter the opposing jaw. Natalie later became the president of the club and an official of the French Rugby Federation! (Robert Natalie was once sent off before a match. Unusually the two teams were coming out through the same tunnel at the same time. Natalie looked across at his opposite number and punched him. The referee sent him off immediately, before he had even got onto the field.)

With three minutes to go and Montchanin leading 15-13, Nick took his team off the field. They all went to the changing room and started to take their boots off.

The Saint-Claude officials came in in great excitement. They had to go back on. Already the side had lost points for the players sent off. They stood to lose another two points for walking off the field.

Back the dejected and humiliated Saint-Claude team trooped onto the field to play out the rest of the match.

They returned to the dressing room and there they sat, hands over eyes sobbing. Dave was astonished, even more astonished to see his brother behaving in like manner. Nick looked out from under his hand, caught Dave's eye and winked, encouraging him to do likewise. Dave followed suit.

MALLETT FAMILY COLLECTION

For Saint-Claude! Nick charges in the snow. His brother Dave is second right.

Suddenly, as if at a signal, the sobbing stopped, wine bottles were opened and the players were soon singing in the shower.

It was not easy at Saint-Claude. The locals wanted victory and were more impressed by it than by the division in which their team played. They did not realise how tough it was when Mallett took the team up into the first division. Mallett's fourth year was a bad one when they lost four home matches and five of the senior players gave up. Their players, many of whom had menial jobs in the area, were mainly local men as they did not have the money to pay players from elsewhere.

Then Mallett organised a coup d'etat, got rid of the president of Saint-Claude and brought in some new players. That year, 1989, they played in the final of the second division in Montchanin. Little Saint-Claude, with its population of 13 000, sent 32 bus-loads and four trainloads of people, with drum and bugle, to the match.

Saint-Claude lost 18-9 to ASPTT, the telecommunications team from Paris, but the people went back happy to Saint-Claude. They made Nick Mallett a freeman of the town in the big marquee they had erected in the town square. In Saint-Claude Nick Mallett reigned. But the Saint-Claudians were not always as generous. The crowd was partisan and often unpleasant, so much so that Jane and Karen stopped going to matches after a while. If the team won, they would be immediately served at the shop and given free baguettes. If the team had lost, they struggled to get served at all.

PARIS

After five years, with two small children, Nick and Jane packed up to come home.

Nick was surprised to receive a phonecall from Christian Leothier of AC Boulogne-Billancourt, a club in Paris near the Bois de Boulogne, opposite a Louis XIV hunting lodge. He asked Nick to do for his club what he had done for Saint-Claude. Nick explained that there were financial considerations of a serious kind and that his business of running the bistro brought him in some fr. 30 000 per month. There was no point in considering a journey to Paris unless that was the figure to discuss. Leothier was not put off by it.

Mallett went to Paris and, French style, met the club president and a player from the club's financial committee for lunch. It was soon apparent that they did not have the money and were embarrassed. Mallett said that he was enjoying the lunch but that there was no further point in discussing the matter. He was not going to beat about the bush. Then Leothier came in and it was clear to Mallett and the club men that he would make up the shortfall. Mallett was to stay for a year. A year became four years.

It was in Paris that he really developed his coaching. Gone was the pressure of making a business work and being under pressure to win matches to help it along. Now he could dedicate his time to coaching.

Some of the more glamorous clubs in Paris were Racing Club de Paris and PUK, the Paris University club. He recruited players, brought in disciplines such as attendance at practices, got them fit and instilled into them spirit and pride. Soon they were doing well.

He also introduced the rolling maul to French rugby which loved flair more than force. On one occasion his side took a kick-off and rolled some 60 metres down the field to score two minutes later.

Mallett was more successful in Paris than at Saint-Claude. But already a tendency had started. He had taken Saint-Claude to promotion. He took AC Boulogne-Billancourt (AC BB) to promotion and he was to do rehabilitation jobs on False Bay, then Boland and then, gloriously, the Springboks. His departure from the clubs and Boland led to their decline. In 1998 Saint-Claude were in the French Nationale 1 (third division), AC BB in Nationale 3 (fifth division). In 1998 False Bay were in the second division and in 1999 Boland were in serious trouble.

In Nick's first season with AC BB, when he was the top try-scorer in the French second division, he took his team to the promotion match. They drew 19-all with Strasbourg but were not promoted. Both teams had the same number of tries and had goaled the same number of kicks. But all Strasbourg's kicks had been penalties and two of AC Boulogne-Billancourt's had been drop goals. By some bizarre bit of philosophy a penalty was regarded as better than a dropped goal and so Strasbourg were promoted.

Mallett was all set to go home, but the club begged him to stay. The club found more money, Mallett stayed on, but his family returned to South Africa. It was a good six months for his coaching, but because of the separation, a bad one for his family life. His last year was the best one as AC Boulogne-Billancourt competed with top clubs such as Tarbes, PUK, Béziers, Begles and Bordeaux.

Mallett took AC Boulogne-Billancourt to a semi-final in the 1991-92 season, which they lost to the University of Lyon 21-18 at Stade Gerland. Lyon's president, Robert Bourachot, was also the managing director of the water company Lyonnaise des Eaux, which employed rugby players as 'water inspectors'. Bourachot was later gaoled for producing false invoices and embezzling funds which he was diverting to political parties as a way of getting contracts with local and regional authorities.

The first part of their stay in Paris was great for Nick and Jane. The children were at nursery school and they had time for themselves in a comfortable apartment. Jane really came into her own there. She had a part-time job in the afternoons and Nick did much of the child minding.

Jane returned home with the children but when Nick's short stay was being extended, eventually to two years, she went back to join him. Their accommodation, near the Bois de Boulogne, was cramped. And yet they had a cosy time and made good friends with four other couples from the rugby club.

One of the advantages for the family living in France was learning another language. Nick had listened to French lessons on tapes before going to France and Jane had studied French at university. By the end of their stay they were both comfortable in the beautiful language. Kate started school in France and was speaking French fluently when they returned. She has since gone for weekly tuition to keep up her French. Because Dougie was so young, he had not really started to learn French by the time they returned home.

HOME AGAIN

Due to come home, Mallett needed a job. He applied for the Western Province coaching job for 1994 as the successor to Dawie Snyman, but it was given to Alan Zondagh instead. Zondagh was the Villager coach in 1993 and coached Western Province from 1993 to 1996, after which Harry Viljoen became the coach for a year and then Alan Solomons.

Mallett thought of teaching at Bishops, his father's own school, and spoke about it to Tim Hamilton-Smith, his coach when he started at UCT. There appeared not to have been an opening at the school just then but another opportunity followed.

False Bay, an embattled first division club in the Western Province, were looking for a coach. Butch Watson-Smith, the chairman of False Bay, approached first Basil Bey and then Tim Hamilton-Smith, both Bishops masters and both former False Bay players. They both turned the offer down. Then Hamilton-Smith suggested Mallett to Watson-Smith and phoned Nick in Paris to tell him to expect a call. Watson-Smith spoke to Rob van der Valk, the accountant/businessman who was chairman of False Bay and keen on lifting his club from the doldrums. Van der Valk telephoned Mallett in Paris on Christmas day and again on New Year's Day in 1994. It was the start of an excellent relationship.

Eventually they agreed to terms and Mallett was happy to accept the coaching job at False Bay. The salary was R40 000 for the season, which Van der Valk thought enormous but which he paid. It was a toe in the coaching door. Nick's main job, however, was working with his sister Tessa in her marketing business.

Having accepted, Mallett was soon in action. He wanted a good player to organise his backs. He suggested Mike Bayly, who was the Villager captain at the time. Bayly, a former Matie, had played for Western Province at centre and fullback, a strong, clever player. Mallett phoned him from Paris and Bayly eventually agreed to change clubs. He became the False Bay captain. This, too, was the start of a good relationship, as Bayly went with Mallett to Boland, which he captained, and succeeded Mallett as Boland coach. A special bond exists between captain and coach.

Mike Bayly said: 'Nick Mallett is the best coach I ever played under. He has remarkable knowledge of rugby and is intelligent. Secondly he is honest. Everybody knows where he stands with Nick. And he was part of the team at Boland. He would run and have fun with the team.'

False Bay RFC, some 80 years old and founded on the beach at Muizenberg in 1929, was in the southern part of the Cape Peninsula. Villagers, closer to the centre of Cape Town, had been a club of greater glamour till False Bay won the Grand Challenge Cup of the Western Province in 1974. Mallett coached them in 1994 and 1995.

In 1993, the year before Mallett took over, False Bay came 12th out of 20 teams in Western Province's first division and in 1994 11th out of 20. The first division was due to be split into two sections of ten teams each, with False Bay going into the second division, but they avoided the drop only because the first was enlarged to 12 teams. (In the Western Province, the names of the divisions are different, such as Super

Leagues and Premier Leagues, but they amount to first and second division.) In 1995 there were ten teams in the first division and False Bay came fourth. In 1996 Nick left and False Bay came 9th out of 10 teams, not just because Mallett had left but also because he took several good players with him. They were not demoted that year because the league was increased to 12 teams, but in 1997 they were 11th out of 12 teams and demoted.

In 1995 Nick Mallett played his last game of rugby for False Bay. It was not a glorious ending, as he was sent to the cooler for standing on a UCT player. He said afterwards that he was actually trying to step over the player but that it was not so easy at his advanced age. He was then just short of 39 years of age. He stood behind the posts at the Philip Herbstein Ground in Constantia, shouting instructions to his team. Twice they joined him behind the posts when UCT, his old club, scored, and he gave them pep talks. But in truth it was not a dignified occasion.

1995 was the last year of 'amateur' rugby, however shamateur it had been. Now there was naked professionalism and vast changes in the laws of the game. Rugby was a whole new ball game, in the boardroom and off the field. Mallett relished the change.

BOLAND

'Let's go to Boland,' Rob van der Valk said.

'You must be mad,' said Nick Mallett.

Rob van der Valk gave his reasons. He did not have the resources to contract the 25 players False Bay would need to win the Grand Challenge. He had been in a conversation with Johan van der Merwe, the Northerns TC hooker, and Johnny Trytsman, who was playing for False Bay, and they were considering joining Boland, the huge country area around Western Province.

Mallett, Van der Valk, Van der Merwe and Trytsman met in Kirstenbosch, the National Botanical Gardens on the slopes of Table Mountain, and Mallett was persuaded to apply for the job, which he did.

Mallett and Van der Valk met Jackie Abrahams, the Boland president, in the Spur Restaurant in Paarl. They had met when the Springboks were in France in 1992, and had got on well. There was no doubt that Mallett would get the job even though Boland went ahead with the formalities of advertising the post.

In 1996 Mallett went to coach Boland, taking with him several False Bay players and Rob van der Valk as his manager to look after contracts and logistics. Certain people had expected him to coach Western Province, but when he went to Boland and with a few False Bay players, he incurred wrath in some quarters and was snubbed by Ronnie Masson, the president of the Western Province RFU. With typical forthrightness Mallett then wrote to Masson to express his annoyance at being snubbed. Masson apologised.

Mallett has ever been a man to make administrators queasy, for he challenges them by cutting to the essence of their function. And so his stay at Boland was not without confrontation with officialdom.

The Boland coach weighing his words.

The All Blacks were coming to South Africa in 1996, at the time when Mallett was coaching Boland. Their itinerary included matches against Eastern Province, Griqualand West and the Boland Invitation XV. Mallett protested, wanting his union to have the same privilege of playing as a province against the All Blacks. The status quo remained and he chose two non-Boland players for the Invitation XV. One of them was Breyton Paulse on the wing, the other Cobus Visagie at prop.

The Boland executive wanted him to select MacNiel Hendricks on the wing as well, but Mallett refused. After all his kicker, Francois Horn, was on the other wing and he did not want to replace his talented young fullback, Marius Goosen, the spark to many Boland moves.

The Boland executive then wrote Mallett a stern letter complaining that they had not been listened to. It was signed by the president, Jackie Abrahams. Nick Mallett, never short of words, went off to Tim Brukman, his lawyer friend, and they produced a seven-page reply. In it, they pointed out that the verbal contract, to which Rooies van Wyk, the former president of the Boland Rugby Union, had been a witness, was binding, and that by that contract Mallett was to have a free hand in choosing his team.

The Boland executive apologised and unconditionally withdrew their complaint.

The problem, in Mallett's view, had arisen because they had not grasped the full implications of professionalism and the changed rôle of the coach. They were amateurs who loved rugby, and, like all lovers of the game, they fancied themselves as selectors and aspirant coaches. They expected the coach to listen to them. But the paid coach was no longer going to listen to amateur officials, however well meaning they were. He was going to work out the budget, recruit players, see to their contracts and pick his team. After all, he carried the final can, which was success or failure on the field of play.

Mallett believed that administrators should administrate, coaches coach and players play – but all with the same goal in mind – the success of the game within their jurisdiction. In South African rugby there was too much of the 'them and us' divide between administrators on the one hand and players and coaches on the other.

The problem was a common one throughout the rugby world as the game dragged itself into professionalism. Sadly, Boland did not really learn and Mallett's successor, Mike Bayly, suffered in the same unhappy way.

Boland, founded in 1939 from Western Province, has been very much the country cousin to Western Province, but suddenly they became competitive, with a positive attitude, as they embraced professionalism.

In 1995, when there were still 22 rugby unions in South Africa, Boland did not compete for the Currie Cup. They were in the third group of provinces, Central B, and came third in that section, behind South Eastern Transvaal and Vaal Triangle. That meant that there were 13 unions above them and 8 below them.

In 1996, when there were 14 unions and all competed for the Currie Cup, the preliminary rounds were in two sections. Boland came fourth out of seven, behind Natal, Golden Lions and Mpumalanga.

One of their best performances was in 1996 against the All Blacks in Worcester before a crowd of 25 000. The All Blacks led 24-0 at half time after Breyton Paulse had been tackled at the corner after a 40-metre run for the goal-line. But Paulse did score before he was replaced by burly MacNiel Hendricks. In all, Boland scored three tries and were down just 24-21 till a penalty and a last-minute try gave the All Blacks victory, 32-21.

Afterwards, Mallett was disappointed!

In 1997 the 14 unions were all in a single league, and Boland ended seventh, a point behind Griquas and two points behind Northern Transvaal, scoring 66 tries in their 13 matches. Only the Free State Cheetahs, Natal Sharks, Gauteng Lions and Western Province scored more tries.

In 1996 Marius Goosen had been Boland's main try scorer, with 6 tries. In 1997 it was Stefan Terblanche, with 13 tries, second only to Jan-Harm van Wyk.

It was Mallett's big disappointment that Boland did not reach a semi-final under him. In 1997 they needed just one more win to make it. They lost to the Gauteng Lions by two points when the Zimbabwean referee Martie Wiles awarded the Lions a penalty try, for which he later apologised. Boland lost to Western Province by a point when Louis Koen kicked a conversion on the stroke of time. And they lost to Northern Transvaal in Pretoria when Roland de Marigny kicked the winning drop goal at the final whistle.

Nick Mallett enjoyed his coaching at Boland. 'The guys at Boland have great fun. We have a great team spirit and that inspires great loyalty. It is important to get team spirit going. Guys must want to play.' Mallett was not an aloof coach, afraid that familiarity would lead to contempt. He was part of the team and partied with the team after matches.

At the end of 1996 André Markgraaff got Mallett into the Springbok coaching structure.

SPRINGBOK DUTY

The new South Africa had enjoyed two joyful events – the first democratic elections of 1994 and the victory in the Rugby World Cup in 1995, when the rainbow nation, a bud in 1994, seemed to burst into a radiant flower. The whole nation rejoiced. The heroic trinity of all this were Nelson Mandela, the country's esteemed president, Kitch Christie, the calm, personable Springbok coach, and François Pienaar, the blond Springbok captain with his faced laced in blood in his nation's cause. Soon only one hero would remain.

First Kitch Christie, suffering from a horrible blood disorder, became too ill to continue and in came André Markgraaff, taciturn and saturnine, but acceptable – as long as the Springboks continued to be victorious.

THE 1996 TOUR

Never has there been a more inauspicious start to a tour. The whole of 1996 had been wracked with controversy till the nation was shrieking its rage, most of it directed at the Springbok coach, André Markgraaff. The euphoria of 1995 had plunged into hysteria. The cause was not just defeat.

At the start, South Africa beat the awkward Fijians and then went off, world champions, to visit the recently vanquished in the Antipodes. They went full of hope. They limped back.

The Wallabies beat the Springboks in a match which the Springboks threw away. They went further south to New Zealand on a day of merciless weather, and even more merciless refereeing, and lost to the boot of Andrew Mehrtens.

Uneasiness reigned in the Springbok camp but they were consoled by the thought that the Antipodeans would have to play in South Africa. 'Wait until we get them on the Highveld,' we said. The Wallabies were decent about it and lost in Bloemfontein. But the All Blacks came, saw and conquered – first in the Tri-Nations and then in the tour series, the first All Blacks to win a series in South Africa, 40 years after the All Blacks had first won a series off the Springboks, 59 years after the Springboks had been the first team ever to win a series in New Zealand, which was also the first series win in rugby contests between the two countries.

There was controversy – about the old South African flag which die-hards waved in Bloemfontein, to which the Springbok response was ambiguous; about the sacking of James Small for extracurricular ill-discipline; and about Os du Randt's leaving the field because, so he said, he was *gatvol* (brassed off). But above all there was defeat, bitter and comprehensive. The nation was plunging into acrimonious gloom.

And then came the selection of the Springbok team to tour Argentina, France and Wales. First the announcement was botched when the nation waited for the broadcast

1996: Touring can be tiring! Kobus Wiese and James Dalton catch up on sleep.

and the deadline was missed. When the announcement was eventually made, it astonished, dismayed and angered: François Pienaar, hero and icon, was omitted. Fury unbridled shrieked across the nation. There were phone-ins, there were newspaper articles. Everywhere the name of André Markgraaff, the solemn coach from Kimberley, was vilified.

Somehow he went on, doing what he believed was right.

He started by gathering his own management team. Mallett, too, was to realise the importance of gathering the right team about him. He knew what he wanted, or rather what he did not want. He did not want his players to be treated as management had treated him when he was a player.

Markgraaff realised fully that the change in the Laws of the Game after 1995 had altered the game. The style of play that had won the Springboks the 1995 World Cup would simply not suit the new game. The Natal style of play, he believed, suited the Springboks best. He could not have Natal's Ian McIntosh in his team, because of Ian's tiff with Louis Luyt, but he could have Hugh Reece-Edwards who was coaching the Natal backs. He needed a coach of the backs in any case and the Natal way promised excitement. After all, the four Natal outside backs – wings, outside centre and fullback – had scored nearly 100 tries in 1996.

The choice of Reece-Edwards, bizarrely enough, caused ructions in Natal where he stood accused of giving the Springboks the Natal recipe, presumably because they regarded their provincial interests as greater than those of South Africa. The same criticism was levelled at Alan Solomons when he was helping Harry Viljoen, the Western Province coach, and then also became assistant to Nick Mallett. Markgraaff's main lieutenant was Mallett, who, he believed, was the best coach of forwards in the country. That meant that the coaching style was likely to be the Natal-Boland-Griqua way. All three provinces tended to play the same brand of a fast, direct, 15-man game.

In addition, Markgraaff appointed the inexperienced (at least in coaching terms) Carel du Plessis to add variety of thought to the coaching staff, especially in the development of individual skills and decision-making, and to add flair to the game plan. It did not quite work out.

Markgraaff, Mallett and Du Plessis had played together in Western Province teams.

In the wake of the Pienaar hysteria, the team met in Pretoria to prepare for the trip. Other problems arose. Some of the players had lucrative World Cup contracts and some did not, a bone of contention that added much to the misery of 1996. When the Springboks visited the Ferrari factory in November 1997, Gary Teichmann, the Springbok captain who had not been in the World Cup squad, was asked if he would buy one and replied: 'Hell, no. Only World Cup players can afford these.' This needed urgent sorting out. There was also disaffection amongst many players. They had had a hard, disappointing season and did not need to go battling around the world just before Christmas.

The sea change that occurred was remarkable and that same team would return smiling to a heroes' welcome at the end of it all.

Part of this was thanks to the team-centred management style. The players were to be 'treated as adults', a frequent enough cry, and they would have much self-responsibility. It started right at the beginning of the tour. The team were set to leave on the long flight from Johannesburg to Buenos Aires, flying business class, but it was 23 seats short. Some benefited by being upgraded to first class, but some would have to travel economy class.

Then Nick Mallett said: 'Let's set a precedent. Let the whole of the management travel at the back.'

The entire management agreed. It set the tone for the tour. The management was there for the sake of the players who are, after all, the most important people.

ARGENTINA

The tour was a particularly happy one, made easier by the team's success and because the players were given the opportunity to fulfil themselves and take responsibility. They were also fortunate in that the Argentinian part of the tour was splendid. The players were well accommodated, the steak was marvellous, the weather was great, their hosts gentlemanly and hospitable, the rugby was not too demanding, and the players discovered BA News, the huge discotheque in Buenos Aires.

Already in Argentina the team was split into two. The test team was chosen and would remain intact for all five tests on the tour. Mallett came more and more to take charge of the Dirt Trackers, as the mid-week team called themselves.

Both teams went up the Paraná River to Rosario and enjoyed the wonderful facilities of the Jockey Club and victory in a free-flowing opening match under lights at the Duendes Club where special seating had been organised at the neat ground. On the next day, which had started in burning heat, both teams travelled through a storm that closed the airports and turned roads into rivers, back across the pampas to Buenos Aires and the Claridge Hotel near Avenida Florida. It was a day of dramatic weather.

The first test was played in heat at Ferro Carril Oeste Stadium, and then the teams split. The Dirt Trackers, under Mallett, went off to Mendoza at the foot of the Andes, while the test team stayed on in Buenos Aires with Markgraaff. Half of the management team moved into the Plaza Hotel in Mendoza. Markgraaff joined the Dirt Trackers only on the day of the match, which was a runaway victory for the Springboks against their provincial opposition. Breyton Paulse scored five tries in his début match for the Springboks.

Results in Argentina:

South Africa	45	Rosario	36
South Africa	46	Argentina	15
South Africa	89	Cuyo	19
South Africa	44	Argentina	21

ON TO FRANCE

The coaching pattern was set in Argentina, and Mallett continued to run the Dirt Trackers, who developed such astonishing spirit that one of the players, Garry Pagel, said that he had never played in any other team with equivalent spirit. The two teams flew from the heat of Buenos Aires to snow in Paris and an uncomfortable stay in Brive on the western edge of the Massif Central – without doubt their least favourite stop on the tour. The players found their location cold, inhospitable and remote.

Although both teams were in Brive, Mallett was having an almost complete say in the running of the mid-week team. It had been presumed that the test team would play against the French Barbarians, but the Trackers again did duty and lost.

Their defeat was due partly to the Barbarians' creative use of the ball, partly to their own bumbling and partly to jetlag, which stayed with the team for quite some time.

After Brive the test team went with Markgraaff and Reece-Edwards to Bordeaux to prepare for the first test while Mallett took the Trackers to a remote location outside of Lyon. Jetlag was still prevalent. Sleeping was a problem as the circadian rhythms had been disturbed.

The players were amazed at Mallett's relentless energy through it all. On a cold day when there was snow around and the prospect of a long journey to where they would practise, the players decided to knock their coach out and slipped four sleeping pills into his food at lunchtime. They watched in wonderment as Mallett's energy refused to flag – through the team talk and the bus journey and the practice. Then to their relief he dozed off briefly on the bus home, waking to declare: 'I don't know why you people are having a problem sleeping. I'm having no problems at all.' The team was relieved. Mallett was, possibly, human after all.

This time Markgraaff did not make the match, but stayed in Bordeaux with his team for fear of being snowbound and unable to return to Bordeaux. He listened to a commentary of the Dirt Trackers' match provided by Koos de Beer, the team's administrator, over a cellphone.

In the great soccer stadium of Lyon, Stade de Gerland, which was being revamped for the soccer World Cup, the Springboks played exceptionally well in the cold and driving rain to score five tries to two and won 36-20. Their opponents were a 'selection' team, purportedly from south-east France but in fact from all over France.

In this match Krynauw Otto, an almost ignored lock as Kobus Wiese and Mark Andrews secured their places in the test team, excelled. Mallett seemed to get the best out of him, and there was even better to come when Mallett later chose him for the Springbok team as an ideal lock – massive, mobile and capable of big tackles.

Mallett, of course, was very much at home in France. Repeatedly, old rugby friends came to see him. He changed the Springboks' Paris hotel to the Concorde Lafayette. He organised his old club, AC Boulogne-Billancourt, to provide practice facilities in the Bois de Boulogne. And he made speeches. After the Barbarians' match he did the French the courtesy of speaking in French, and most speeches, of which there were many, were in French. After the Bordeaux test he produced a great piece of diplomatic finesse.

Bernard Lapasset, the president of the French Rugby Federation, who speaks excellent English, spoke in praise of the Springboks' convincing victory, but solely in French. Mallett replied and in his voluble French thanked the president for his hospitality and his generous praise of the Springboks. Then he went on to say that his kind words would have been much appreciated by the Springboks if they could have understood them. He further suggested that it would be good for future relationships between the two countries if, at least, an interpreter was provided on such occasions.

The French, who generally hero-worshipped Mallett, applauded the finesse.

Mallett was not always diplomatic. The Trackers' last match was bizarre – played in Lille with Pablo Deluca of Buenos Aires to referee. Deluca issued a flood of penalties against the Springboks, and some controversial decisions, aided by intervention from the touch judges. The Springboks lost a match they were never going to be allowed to win. The university side, student champions of the world, celebrated greatly, joined by the touch judges.

Mallett let it be known that he was unhappy with the performance of the officials and with some of the violence on the field of play. When a student arrived to swop jerseys, Mallett showed him the door. His rage was obvious and in sharp contrast to his acceptance of defeat in Brive.

The Springboks won again at Parc des Princes, to complete a rare pair of victories on a tour of France. The Wallabies had never achieved it. The last team to win both tests in France had been the All Blacks in 1990. After that, the Wallabies, the Springboks and the All Blacks had failed to do so.

Results in France:

Barbarians Françaises	30	South Africa	22
South Africa	36	Sélection du Sud-Est	20
South Africa	22	France	12
France Universitaire	20	South Africa	13
South Africa	13	France	12

WALES

For many, life became easier in Wales, with a familiar language and food, and the relaxed welcome which the men of Wales afforded. After the Paris win, Markgraaff promised his men the week off. As they got out of the bus, late on the Sunday night, Gary Teichmann went to him and said: 'Coach, the guys want to practise.'

And so the Cardiff week became much like other weeks on tour.

The Welsh match, on a Sunday, was a great triumph for the Springboks as they played their most relaxed and, possibly as a result, their best rugby of the tour. The star turn was Joost van der Westhuizen who became the first player in history to score a hat-trick of tries at Cardiff Arms Park.

Result:

South Africa	37	Wales	20

1997

Markgraaff and Mallett spent time planning 1997, which started with fitness testing in Cape Town. The first setback was when Johan Ackermann, a lock of enormous potential, tested positive for the use of a banned substance and was suspended for two years. Markgraaff had everything in place for the new season, including the appointment of the same management team. All of this came tumbling down when what became known as the 'Bester tape' became public in February: a voice, clearly Markgraaff's, was heard making derogatory and racist remarks about many people on a tape made clandestinely by André Bester, the former Griqua captain. Markgraaff immediately resigned in tears.

These were hard times for SARFU. There was this scandal. There was the ongoing government inquiry into SARFU's affairs and there was the universal unpopularity of Louis Luyt. In the midst of all this came the bombshell of the Markgraaff resignation for the worst possible reasons in South Africa – racist insult.

Nick Mallett was an obvious contender for the post, but it was known that SARFU was worried about him. After all, he was a man who would have his say – loudly.

They went for the quiet man with no coaching qualifications, Carel du Plessis, one of the greatest Springboks of all time, the gliding Prince of Wings. Appointing him as the Springbok coach was a disastrous choice. Under him, the Springboks scored nine tries to three but lost in a bizarre series against the mediocre Lions, which caused vast rejoicing and raucous crowing in the Home Unions. They were also smashed by the All Blacks and ended the year dispirited, despite a massive win over the dilapidated Wallabies.

It was small consolation but some recognition for Mallett that he was given the job of coaching the Emerging Springboks for their match against the Lions at Boland Stadium in Wellington on the Tuesday before the first test at Newlands. There was obviously hardly any time to get things right with the pick-up team he was handed, and the Lions duly gave the Emerging Springboks a drubbing: 51-22. The Lions' Tim Stimpson scored 26 points and Nick Beal three tries. The score was 16-15 to the Lions at half-time but in the second half the Lions' backs were rampant. Their task was made easier as all the Emerging Springboks were given a game.

None of the Emerging Springboks had ever been Springboks, but some did become Springboks, some in more sensible positions.

THE EMERGING SPRINGBOKS: MJ Smith (replaced by Kayalethu Malotana), Deon Kayser, Percy Montgomery, MacNiel Hendricks, Paul Treu, Louis van Rensburg (replaced by Marius Goosen), Jopie Adlam (replaced by Kat Myburgh), Jaco Coetzee, Phillip Smit, Warren Brosnihan (replaced by Trevor Arendse), Braam Els, Ryno Opperman, Niel du Toit, Dale Santon (captain) (replaced by Jannie Brooks), Robbie Kempson (replaced by Lourens Campher).

THE LIONS: Tim Stimpson, John Bentley, Allan Bateman, Will Greenwood, Nick Beal, Mike Catt, Austin Healey, Tony Diprose, Neil Back, Rob Wainwright, Jim Davidson, Nigel Redman, Jason Leonard (captain), Mark Regan, Graham Rowntree.

Nick Mallett, the successful and energetic Springbok coach, in 1998.

THE COACH

Michael Owen-Smith wrote in 1997: 'It is almost as though Nick Mallett has that sixth sense that makes the difference between the superficial and the true rugby visionary.' This was when Carel du Plessis was the Springbok coach and Nick Mallett was coaching Boland. It was a year in which things happened with nighmarish haste. André Markgraaff had started as the Springbok coach. On 14 February there were rumours of the Bester tape. On 19 February Markgraaff resigned. On 24 February SARFU announced the appointment of Carel du Plessis as the coach. Springbok rugby, recently under Markgraaff, plummeted downwards.

A few months after Owen-Smith had written the above, Mallett rode onto the scene, the St George to slay the dragon of defeat, the cavalry to rescue the Springboks from ignominy. Soon he became one of the most popular men in South Africa.

Just before the announcement of Carel du Plessis as the Springbok coach, Rian Oberholzer, SARFU's chief executive officer, phoned Mallett to tell him that SARFU had been faced with a choice between him and Du Plessis but had decided on Du Plessis. SARFU hoped that they would be able to use Mallett's expertise in the future. Mallett told Oberholzer that he was disappointed and that he could not work with Du Plessis as their personalities and rugby methods were too different. If they were to work together and the team lost, it would be possible that Mallett could be accused of undermining Du Plessis. Oberholzer asked if Du Plessis could phone Mallett.

Du Plessis phoned some five days later and told Mallett that he had been thinking about his management team. Mallett congratulated him and said that he really did not think it a good idea that he should assist Du Plessis. Gert Smal would suit Du Plessis better. He also told Du Plessis that he was amazed that he had accepted the job as he had no coaching experience.

There was no bitterness in the conversation. Mallett wished him well and later sent him a letter of good wishes as well.

At the time, Mallett wrote that he and Hugh Reece-Edwards would have found it difficult to work under Du Plessis. 'He has his vision and we have ours. I wouldn't have asked Carel to assist me had I been offered the post. I would've liked to work with Hugh.' (Later, when he was in charge, Mallett opted not to use Hugh Reece-Edwards.)

Carel du Plessis coached the Springboks, Mallett Boland. In retrospect, Mallett will say that it all turned out for the best. Du Plessis took over a rehabilitated Springbok team and plunged them into the depths of humiliation and uncertainty. Mallett worked with the Boland team, gaining experience and respect.

By August, an unhappy six months after Carel du Plessis had been appointed, it was clear that he had to go. It was also clear that Nick Mallett, the man SARFU did not want, was the obvious choice for the job. Support for Mallett soon proved 100 per cent right.

Carel du Plessis, who had ignored players like André Joubert, Henry Honiball and James Small, and had played others out of position in a side that became increasingly dispirited and unsure, was dismissed after addressing the SARFU executive at Ellis Park on 30 August 1998, ironically in the wake of his team's one good performance of the year – their record victory over the Wallabies in the last Tri-Nations match, thus saving the Springboks from carrying off the wooden spoon.

The ground swell in favour of Mallett became a tidal wave as respected coaches such as André Markgraaff and Harry Viljoen gave him public support. Markgraaff said: 'I believe Nick is the best man for the job and very capable of turning round the season. He has my full support.' Ian McIntosh described him as 'a young coach who has a vision of the modern game'.

The three coaches whom Mallett most admired were André Markgraaff, Harry Viljoen and Ian McIntosh.

Rob Louw, his team-mate and early rival, said: 'Nick's a complete competitor and that's got to be an A-plus factor for SA rugby.' Morné du Plessis and Divan Serfontein, both former Springbok captains, supported his candidature.

Barry Glasspool, the respected rugby writer, added his weight, saying: 'When Nick Mallett talks, people listen.' The *Sunday Tribune* called him 'a tough man for a tough job'.

Dan Retief of the *Sunday Times*, a much awarded rugby writer, was more cautious: 'South African rugby could be heading for another period of disaster, unless urgent steps are taken ahead of the Springboks' tour to Italy, France, England and Scotland at the end of the year. The way things stand, South Africa's new coach – whoever is appointed on September 25 to take over from Carel du Plessis – is on a hiding to nothing.'

Mercifully the doom of his prophecy, which reflected the general mood of South African rugby at the time, was averted as Nick Mallett rode in, smiling, confident and successful.

Wynand Claassen, Springbok captain in 1981 when Mallett was a young player, was more optimistic when he said: 'If Mallett can convince the country that he is the right man for the job and get his Springboks to perform with greater consistency, he will make South Africa again a rugby power.'

Mallett achieved both – quickly and effectively, a Caesar of the rugby field who came, had a brief look and conquered.

Despite the general support for Mallett, SARFU chose to go through some new motions of its own, calling for applications for the post, suggesting that they were going about things in a professional way. Amongst names mentioned were Dick Marks of Australia and Barry Wolmarans. There were 39 applicants, partially giving the lie to Mallett's later statement: 'The opportunity to coach the Boks was there and there weren't many people keen on the job.' Despite speculation, Ian McIntosh was not an applicant. He would not apply as long as Louis Luyt was president of SARFU. Harry Viljoen of Western Province had also had a tiff with Luyt and was not in contention. SARFU were not at all interested in employing a foreign coach.

For the job, which Barry Newcombe of *The Sunday Times* of London described as 'the most fragile heritage in international rugby', Mallett had to present his case to the presidents of the 14 unions and SARFU's four executive members.

Mallett said: 'It mattered to me to get the job, because I loved rugby and I thought that I was capable of doing it as well as anyone else, but only under my own conditions – that I was appointed until the end of the next World Cup; there would be no interference from the executive in the running of the side; that I could appoint my own management team; and that I would have the final say in selection.'

Mallett delayed his application for the job by ten days to make sure that his conditions were known and accepted. He would select his own team and his own management team – without interference from any other body. And he would do it until the end of the 1999 Rugby World Cup.

He was early for his 11.30 am interview, punctual as always. But SARFU's executive was going on and on with another meeting. Mallett presumed, despairingly, that it was another interviewee on the short-list.

He went for a walk along a passage and came across Anthony Mackaiser, SARFU's pressman, who was typing. Mackaiser asked Mallett how one spelt Hertfordshire. Mallett did it for him, and said: 'Funny. That's where I was born.'

'I know,' said Mackaiser. 'I'm typing the press release of your appointment.'

There was no short-list, no previous interviewee. The interview was delayed as SARFU's executive discussed the Braude Commission of Inquiry into rugby!

Mallett went into the meeting with great confidence to discuss his plans and to put forward his four conditions, the same four he had always put at club level to give himself the freedom to do his job properly.

It is no wonder that Archie Henderson of the *Cape Argus* broke the 'news' of Mallett's appointment the day before the interview!

On 25 September 1997, to everybody's relief and nobody's surprise, SARFU made the announcement that Nick Mallett was the new Springbok coach, the seventh in six years to sip from the 'poisoned chalice' that paid R40 000 a month. He was the third Springbok coach in 1997.

The six coaches preceding Mallett had been John Williams, Gerrie Sonnekus – who did not have the chance to run even a practice as he was forced to resign ahead of a court case in which he was charged with misappropriation of funds during the Free State centenary, a charge which was dismissed – Ian McIntosh, sacked after the 1994 tour to New Zealand, Kitch Christie, who gave up for health reasons, André Markgraaff and Carel du Plessis.

Nick Mallett's contract stated that he was appointed until the end of the 1999 Rugby World Cup. But then Ian McIntosh's contract had been truncated and Carel du Plessis would contest the ending of his contract/agreement. The possibility of failure did not even enter Nick Mallett's mind. 'I believe my position is sound until 1999 – unless, of course, I go completely moggy and punch a referee.'

Nick Mallett had just three weeks to prepare for the five-test tour to Europe, three weeks to turn no-hopers into world-beaters. He came in blazing confidence. 'Obviously results come first, but I've got a chance none of the other coaches had.

A COMPARISON OF THE SPRINGBOKS' PERFORMANCES UNDER EACH COACH

	P	W	D	L	Pf	Pa
John Williams (1992)	5	1	0	4	79	130
Gerrie Sonnekus (1994)	0					
Ian McIntosh (1993-94)	12	4	2	6	252	240
Kitch Christie (1994-95)	14	14	0	0	490	191
André Markgraaff (1996)	13	8	0	5	352	260
Carel du Plessis (1997)	8	3	0	5	288	213
Nick Mallett (1997-98)	17	16	0	1	598	230

Rugby has so long been regarded as the preserve of the white man, especially the white Afrikaner man. I would like to help to change that back to 1995 when the whole country felt good about the game, to a position where everybody will be behind us.

'We must be genuine about this, not just put in somebody on the wing for the look of the thing, but help to change the perception of South African rugby.' Mallett's arrival ushered in a gale of fresh air.

Louis Luyt, the difficult president of SARFU, welcomed the new coach warmly. Things had not always been easy between them, especially after Mallett had criticised the president in *SA Rugby* magazine of August 1997.

Mallett was involved in the magazine and had a monthly column, called, appropriately, *Mallett's Mouthpiece*. The article at which Luyt took offence came in the aftermath of the series defeat against the Lions in 1997. To quote the whole article would be too long and quoting portions runs the risk of giving certain aspects additional emphasis whereas the article dealt with South African rugby as a whole. But the 'offensive' sections are important and should be quoted.

Mallett wrote: 'It is unacceptable to lose to the Lions and no amount of shilly-shallying from SARFU or the coaches can cover it up.'

'No matter how hard Rian Oberholzer has worked to try to convince everyone that rugby is professional and liberal, there's a strong perception that the present administration has been a divisive, rather than unifying, influence on South African rugby. Dr Luyt's administrative ability can't outweigh the negative perception that he has created during his reign over South African rugby. There's no doubt that the majority of South African rugby supporters would prefer rugby administered differently.'

'The average age of SARFU's executive is closer to 70 than 40, and surely the time has come to introduce new blood to our administration.'

'We must get national support for our national team. And if the problem starts at the top, then we must recognise and address this fact.'

It was really quite innocuous, but it was enough to have Mallett summoned by Rian Oberholzer, SARFU's chief executive officer who had been the tournament director of the 1995 World Cup and then the CEO of SANZAR, the organisation running rugby competitions between teams from South Africa, New Zealand and Australia. When Oberholzer phoned him to come to a meeting, Nick Mallett made it clear that he was not prepared to be hauled over the coals. Oberholzer insisted that it would be just a discussion of views on the running of rugby football in South Africa. Later, when Mallett did eventually get the Springbok job, he was forbidden, by his contract, to write articles for publication, including for *SA Rugby*.

In an effort to get Mallett back into good books, André Markgraaff helped smooth the way, taking his old team-mate to see Louis Luyt at Ellis Park. Initially Luyt was angry but soon relaxed as Markgraaff told Luyt that he should be big, recognise Carel du Plessis' failure and appoint Mallett as the Springbok coach.

It would appear that Luyt harboured no grudges for, apart from welcoming Mallett when he announced him as the new coach, he said, with great joy after the Tri-Nations victory, that with this coach and this team South Africa would win the 1999 Rugby World Cup. And that was after Luyt had resigned as president of SARFU, in the midst of all the inquiries and court cases and other controversies, and before he resigned as president of the Golden Lions.

Mallett, the Springbok coach, had no problems with Luyt and certainly no interference. Luyt phoned congratulations on occasion and complained that Mallett had not contacted him to tell him how things were going. For the rest there was complete support.

In Mallett's view, Luyt is a genuine rugby man. He sees him first as a real rugby supporter, secondly as an administrator, thirdly as an aspirant coach and fourthly, as is the case with all ardent supporters of a team, a selector. His treatment of coaches has been subject to massive mood swings which are dependent solely on victory and defeat. Every coach was the best until his team was defeated. Then his future was likely to be brief. Ian McIntosh and Dawie Snyman are cases in point, as was even the great Kitch Christie. When Christie took Transvaal to seven Super 12 defeats in eleven matches in 1996, his tenure as the Transvaal coach came to an abrupt end.

Luyt welcomed Mallett. There were many other welcoming noises at Nick Mallett's appointment. Kepler Wessels, the former South African cricket captain, said: 'Nick Mallett is an impressive fellow and hopefully his strength of character will add some stability to a job that has become a laughing stock to the rest of the sporting world.' More important Gary Teichmann, the current Springbok captain, a man of great deeds and few words, said: 'I really rate him as a coach. He understands the modern game. He is strong and he is determined.' And he begged SARFU to leave Mallett in the job till the end of the 1999 Rugby World Cup.

Where had this saviour of South African rugby come from? What were the qualifications which made him a logical choice and a success as the Springbok coach?

There are those who believe that Nick Mallett coached and captained every team he ever played in without actually being appointed to either position! He certainly gave the impression of being in charge of the teams he played for. But he also spent a long time coaching rugby, doing it with a passion as he did everything else in life.

He was first asked to coach a team in 1975. When he was playing for UCT and living at home, home was Bishops. The principal's house is right next to a field called the Sahara, where the Bishops Under 16 team was coached by Tim Hamilton-Smith, an Oxford man who was also coaching the successful UCT Under 20 team. Tim got Nick to help with his Bishops team. It was Hamilton-Smith who, with Basil Bey, the legendary Bishops coach, taught Nick Mallett how to play as an eighth man.

Part of learning to be a coach is to be coached. In his career Mallett had a variety of coaches, in South Africa and abroad. The sheer variety as well as the quality of many of the coaches, plus his intelligent assimilation of his experiences and development of them, made him the outstanding coach he became.

Then Nick and Jane went to Italy, a great experience for them. Mallett played at Rovigo in Northern Italy, the heartland of Italian rugby, in the 1982-83 season. He also taught English for pocket money, but it really was six months of holiday. They were close to Venice, which Jane loved, were regularly lent an apartment there, and the Italians were kind. Mallett learnt a valuable lesson there – give 100 per cent and you will get it back in kindness and generosity.

For quite some time there was a South African connection at Rovigo, the top Italian rugby club. Schalk Burger had been there before Nick Mallett; Gert Smal and Naas Botha would succeed him, and then Tjaart Marais and Tito Lupini when Nelie Smith was the coach.

The Rovigo coach was Nairn McEwan, the Scottish international who had taken over from the legendary Carwyn James of Wales. The captain of the Rovigo side was Fabrizio Sintich who was, ridiculously wonderful to relate, an old boy of Peterhouse. He had been born in Nairobi and after school returned to Italy with his parents, later playing for the Italian national team. The president of the club was Giancarlo Checchinato, now an executive member of the Italian Rugby Federation and the father of Carlo Checchinato who played against the Springboks in 1997. It was Giancarlo's idea that the Springboks should play in Bologna instead of Rome in 1997.

The rugby may not have been that demanding but Mallett, as always, gave of his best. He was also required to coach, but language constraints put a curb on his normal volubility.

His coaching took off when he left South Africa in a huff in 1985, after the fiasco of the 'Springboks' internal tour in the wake of the cancellation of the All Black tour that year. Then he went up into the mountains of eastern France, as a player-coach at Saint-Claude, a second division club which had high hopes of making the first division. In the passionate arenas of French rugby such expectations put enormous pressure on Nick Mallett. He was expected to play and coach them into a higher division, and rugby football was the village's main activity. In addition he was running the bistro, suitably called Café le Club. This was his source of livelihood and that livelihood would be better if the team did better.

He was playing and coaching in France in 1992 when the Springboks toured, a singularly unhappy tour on and off the field. They shared the series but lost to the Emerging French, French Universities and French Barbarians. On this, the first tour after readmission to world rugby, the standard of the Springbok performance was abysmal and humiliating. Off the field there were all sorts of squabbles as the management locked horns with the French. Accusations flew back and forth, many of them occasioned by differences in language and custom. For one thing the liaison man given them by the French Rugby Federation, Jean Gabriel, spoke no English.

Mallett met the team and was astonished at their low morale. 'It shocked me to see what a bad impression the Springboks gave of themselves, not only on the field. The problem was the way they were forced to tour and that they were subject to a dictatorial system. They were unhappy in France and came across as unhappy people.'

In the midst of the controversy, Mallett, fluent in French and knowledgeable about French rugby, was approached by the players and was willing to help them improve a desperate situation. Abé Malan, the former Springbok hooker and at the time the manager and at the centre of much of the controversy, refused his help, reportedly saying: 'Nick Mallett is a troublemaker. He dresses like a Frenchman. He talks like a Frenchman. He even smells like a Frenchman.' Asked about the incident in 1998, Malan had no recollection of the occurrence.

Having done so well as player/coach at Saint-Claude, Mallett was then persuaded to do the same for AC Boulogne-Billancourt. In all he had nine years in France, successful ones but constantly battling to bring weak sides up the ladder.

The same was true when he moved to False Bay for two years in 1994, and when he coached Boland in 1996 and 1997.

Boland, a province once noted for its sturdy forwards, including the famous trio of Kochs in the 1950s, had suffered as country unions tended to. In 1995 there were 22 unions, divided into four sections. Boland came third in the third section, behind South Eastern Transvaal and Vaal Triangle. That was the end of amateur rugby. In 1996 rugby became officially professional and the number of unions in South Africa was reduced to 14. Boland, with the huge area it serves, survived, but now it was playing Currie Cup rugby. Life would be far from gentle.

In both seasons under Mallett Boland did a lot better than expected. In 1997 their position in the middle of the Currie Cup table could have been even better. They should have defeated the Gauteng Lions, Western Province and Northern Transvaal, but in all three cases they were unlucky to lose late in the game by two points, one point and three points respectively. Then they threw away the match against Mpumalanga. In 1997 Boland scored 66 tries in 13 matches and conceded 43. They scored the most bonus points (12) of any team in the Currie Cup.

Mallett's coaching career has been a long one. Astonishingly, in such a volatile position, he has never been sacked! But then Nick Mallett has great attributes as a coach. He has confidence – in his own ability and in that of his players. He believes that his players can beat anybody and he communicates this confidence to his players. He can lift them above themselves.

After the Springboks had won a famous victory over France at Parc des Princes, Gary Teichmann, the captain, said: 'The big difference in the team has been self-belief. The players seem to be playing more as a team.... And all that is due to Nick Mallett.' Mallett's confidence was infectious. Joost van der Westhuizen said: 'If Nick Mallett said the grass was blue, the 1998 Springboks would agree with him.'

85

The weather and the coach – northern hemisphere cold but Nick Mallett fine.

DAVID ROGERS/ALLSPORT

After the Springboks' splendid victory over Scotland in 1997, Rob Wainwright, the home captain and a medical doctor, said: 'I have never encountered a team with such incredible self-belief. They are quite possibly the best side I have ever seen.'

All good coaches are possessed of this kind of self-belief. You will find it in abundance in John Hart of New Zealand, and yet he may not be able to communicate it all that effectively, if the All Blacks' swift loss of confidence in 1998 was anything to go by. South Africans like Ian McIntosh, Ian Kirkpatrick, Kitch Christie, Harry Viljoen and André Markgraaff all have remarkable self-belief. It is hard to imagine a coach without it. The more coaches can communicate this self-belief, the more effective they are. It is better for a team to do the wrong thing in unison and with conviction than the right thing in a haphazard, half-hearted way.

Of all coaches, Nick Mallett has shown self-belief and he never seems insecure or threatened in what he does. Mallett's inspiring self-belief could turn matches.

In 1997 Boland were down 28-6 at half-time against André Markgraaff's Griqua side in Kimberley. Johnny Trytsman tells it: 'Nick spoke to us from the heart. It was, like you know, he was sharing the pain.' Final score: 28-28. Mike Bayly said that at half-time Nick had a few things to say to the team, telling them they were letting themselves down. 'The players had so much respect for Mallett that they did not want to face his wrath. They were like children trying to please their father.'

His sister Tessa, who played hockey for South African schools against a team from Holland in 1970, says of him : 'Nick is the most positive human being I have ever come across. He's extraordinary in that way – seriously confident.'

Mallett says things as they are – directly, loudly, sometimes harshly, but always with obvious honesty and passion. He says: 'It's far better for a player to know where he stands.'

This has not often been the case in South African rugby. Players, traditionally, have read in the newspaper or heard over the radio that they have been dropped. In 1933

Bennie Osler learnt that he was no longer the Springbok captain when he saw the team pinned on the hotel noticeboard. Naas Botha read in the newspaper that Jannie Breedt had replaced him as captain. Much of André Markgraaff's problems started with the non-selection of François Pienaar, national icon, for the 1996 tour without having spoken to Pienaar first. Mallett would talk to them.

Straight after his appointment he talked to several players, including Joost van der Westhuizen who had made no secret of his aversion to Mallett after the 1996 tour. Their relationship changed remarkably after the talk. Joost was in support of Mallett boots and all and became the Springbok vice-captain.

Van der Westhuizen said: 'There are two qualities which make Nick a great coach. The first is his loyalty. He puts you in the team and he stands by you. The second quality is his enthusiasm.'

Nick Mallett is a loyal man. He was loyal as a schoolboy, loyal to the universities he played for, loyal to his province, loyal to the clubs he coached and now loyal to his Springboks who are really his, for he selects them and he coaches them. Loyalty has meant giving them every opportunity to play where they deserve to be.

On the 1996 tour the Springboks picked the same starting line-up for five tests in a row – the longest run ever for the Springboks. The only change came on the replacement bench for the fifth test when Fritz van Heerden damaged a thigh at the practice on the day before the Welsh test.

Mallett has said: 'I believe that a player must play himself out of the side rather than have people dropped willy-nilly.' This loyalty meant sticking to Percy Montgomery and Pieter Rossouw even though they had lost form and confidence during the 1998 Super 12 and keeping Rassie Erasmus when many were clamouring for the more glamorous Bobby Skinstad.

Mallett in turn wanted men who were loyal: 'I like team players. I really get impressed when I see not necessarily the flashy sort of guys, but a guy who really puts himself on the line for his team. Class will come out, but if you get class and passion and commitment, you're getting there.'

Nick Mallett has always been his own boss, able to take the pressures of being boss. 'The pressure comes with the job. I'm not too worried about it. The buck stops with me.'

The buck belongs to the coach. If the team fails, his head rolls. Players stay on, the coach goes. For that reason he must decide and take responsibility for his decisions. 'I said right from the beginning I won't tolerate interference. It's not going to happen. That was one of the conditions of my contract.'

Mallett knew he would get his team right if he got three things right – the choice of the right management team, the selection of the right players in the right positions and playing the right sort of rugby.

In his discussions with SARFU, Nick Mallett got the management team he wanted. 'I didn't make demands, but I said it was important that I appoint the people I need.' He wanted a management team that would serve his needs which meant serving the needs of the players.

The management team he chose was the following:

COACH:	Nick Mallett
ASSISTANT COACHES:	Alan Solomons, Pieter de Villiers
TECHNICAL ADVISER:	Jake White
ADMINISTRATIVE MANAGER:	Rob van der Valk
PRESS OFFICER:	Alex Broun
MEDICAL DOCTOR:	Frans Verster
PHYSIOTHERAPIST:	Lambert Fick
FITNESS TRAINER:	Dan van der Heever
BAGGAGE MASTER:	Ampie le Roux

It would change. In 1998 Dr Wayne Diesel became the physiotherapist, Kevin Stevenson was doing the fitness training and Pieter de Villiers had moved on to other coaching positions.

The management met each morning to set out the day. Alan Solomons had been the coach at UCT. Dave Mallett had been his captain and he had been Dave's bestman when he was married. A lawyer with the firm Sonnenberg, Hofman & Golombik, Solomons took a sabbatical till the end of the 1999 Rugby World Cup to indulge his passion for rugby to the full. After he had become the assistant Springbok coach, and while doing the job, he became the coach of Western Province, and then, in 1999, of the Stormers.

Of him Nick Mallett said: 'Solly has been extremely popular with the players and he has worked tirelessly at keeping us up to date with what the opposition are doing and ensuring that we are ready for each test.'

Mallett saw Solomons as the perfect foil to himself – the organiser and planner.

The practice routine on tour was something like the following:

Monday:	Flush-out
Wednesday:	Game Structure
Thursday:	Captain's Practice

Solomons, well organised and prepared, would run the 1-1½ hours of skill training on the Monday. Mallett would be more dominant on the Wednesday, looking at team and unit skills, improving what had been defective in the previous match and gearing up for the match to come. This, too, would last 1-1½ hours. There was no doubt that Nick Mallett was the coach. And there was no doubt that the players had to do what he wanted them to do. 'I don't care who told you what, you do it my way.'

What happened on Thursdays was up to Gary Teichmann.

On Friday evenings Mallett introduced a new ceremony to the Springboks, where he would hand each player his jersey for the next day's match.

Mallett, Solomons and the technical adviser, Jake White, ran the rugby side of the tour. Jake White, formerly a schoolmaster at Jeppe High in Johannesburg when James

Dalton and Brent Moyle, the Springbok prop, had been at the school, was recommended to Mallett by André Markgraaff. White put into words the players' manual, which contained moves which they were required to study. He would also organise whatever video material was required. White became a SARFU employee.

On Monday evenings Mallett would take his team through the match analysis. Video footage was used for this and Jake White would be required to edit the video so that only the rugby part remained. The analysis of the match would tend to concentrate on the Springboks in a direct but constructive way. Nick Mallett's sense of humour certainly helped to make the post-mortem less traumatic.

Rian Oberholzer, SARFU's CEO.

Whie would also be required to analyse the opposition's last three or four matches. He would collect certain phases of their play – what they did from scrums on attack and on defence, from line-outs on attack and on defence, at kick-offs and so on. Besides that he would prepare tapes for individual players to take away and study.

Joost van der Westhuizen remarked: 'Nick and his staff identify weaknesses in your game and help you to solve them. They don't say, 'Oh, look he can't pass. Let's drop him.' They will call you in and suggest how you can solve the problem.'

Rob van der Valk was the logistics expert – seeing to travel, accommodation and tickets while on tour. Mallett saw him as the key to the team's happiness. After all, he was the man who looked after the players' contracts. SARFU were happy that he should do so and the players had asked him to do so. With him was Ampie le Roux, the best baggage master a team could have.

Doc Verster, a SARFU employee, Wayne Diesel, a diagnostic physiotherapist, and Kevin Stevenson formed what Mallett believed to be the best rugby medical team in the world.

Arthob Petersen, the team's manager, looked after the ceremonial side of things, as well as many social commitments, freeing Mallett and his men to do the job of serving the needs of the team. Petersen was a member of SARFU's executive.

Alex Broun, an Australian settled in Cape Town and a SARFU employee, was the man at the media's beck and call, as well as Nick Mallett's go-between with them and the organiser of interviews.

The SARFU staff did not stint themselves in trying to provide Mallett and his team with everything he needed and, indeed, wanted to ensure success. When Mallett came into the job with a gale of fresh air, the SARFU staff were the ones to manage the ship through the gale by ensuring that it blew in the right direction.

Rian Oberholzer, SARFU's chief executive officer, a man capable of quick decisions, found the money that was needed. Emaré Harper saw to the manifold travel arrangements with endless energy and attention to detail. Lisa Bon, SARFU's public relations officer, increasingly became Mallett's manager, organising his schedule and that of several of the players as well. Steven Roos, who was appointed SARFU's games support director in 1999, saw to the gear which the team took with them, such as clothes, playing togs and presents.

The organisational abilities of Mallett's management team gave the team the reputation of the best organised Springbok team of all time. This would surprise many of Mallett's team-mates from his playing days, remembering him as a particularly disorganised traveller, happy to borrow anything – a razor, even a toothbrush. The organisation of Team Mallett, as the media referred to the whole caravanserai, worked.

Mallett felt it was a balanced team. He wanted a management that could interact with the players, in a way not previously known in South African rugby. As his tenure progressed he found oddly that while the management was getting closer to the players he was becoming more detached, not aloof but not as close as he had been in his Boland days. It was inevitable as the coach held the players' destinies in his hands. They would not want to be seen currying favour and he would want to be detached enough to make a rational decision.

Nick Mallett had the head and heart for the job.

He had the head to plan thoroughly. Tours and practices were thoroughly prepared in advance. In an interview with Dan Retief in early November 1997, not long after he had been appointed, Mallett laid out his plans for 1998. Retief wrote: 'Mallett's belief that South Africa can, and will, retain the Rugby World Cup is infectious and in his quest to create a uniquely South African way of playing he is to seek approval of a number of innovative proposals ahead of next season.'

1998 was seen as a watershed year, as World Cup contracts were due to end in August and leading players could be drawn down the corridor that led to British pounds and, through rugby league, Australian dollars. Mallett's scheme was that SARFU would contract the top 30 players in the country, provide for their financial needs and limit the number of matches they would play to 30. The Super 12 would start in March rather than February. There would again be proper Springbok trials. And at the end of the year two separate teams with their own management would be chosen to tour in the same area, instead of the single, cumbersome 36-player team.

How much of this did he achieve?

The contracts were sorted out and the Springboks were satisfied. The week for sorting out contracts came after the famous victory in Wellington in the Tri-Nations.

Mallett said: 'There were probably 100 million people watching our game. These blokes deserve to be well paid. It is important to keep these players. To do so their contracts have to be competitive with those of other countries. We cannot lose a top player to a club side in England because of the English pound.' By that stage only five of his squad had World Cup contracts – Joost van der Westhuizen, Krynauw Otto, Mark Andrews, James Dalton and Naka Drotské.

He did not get the dates of the Super 12 changed, limit the number of matches – as the provinces still had a say, especially in the Super 12 – have Springbok trials or tour with two separate teams each with its separate management. If he had had his way, the tour at the end of 1998 would have been by the South African Barbarians and not the Springboks.

What he most achieved was that he chose a team which played his way. Mallett understood the modern game. He was playing it at his Paris club, AC Boulogne-Billancourt, before he returned to South Africa. He brought it to the Springboks on the 1996 tour when he spent hours and hours thrashing out the new game plan with André Markgraaff. Together they opted for tries instead of penalties. They would eschew the simple kick at goal for kicking the ball out near the corner flag in the hope of scoring from the line-out. This had many of the conservatives in desperation. After the Springbok second stringers lost to the French Barbarians in Brive in 1996, Louis Luyt phoned to tell them to kick their penalties at goal.

Mallett stuck by his plans. Kick at goal and you get three points. You also concede more than 60 metres, relieving the pressure on your opponents. Kick for the corner flag and you have the option of seven points and the pressure is tight on the opponents.

Mallett's communication skills meant that he has been able to get his game plan across to his players convincingly. What was the game plan?

André Markgraaff used to talk about his game plan and it was used as a stick with which to beat him. Nick Mallett insisted that there was none, though when Clive Woodward, the England coach, said before the England tests that he had no game plan, Mallett said that he was talking rubbish. 'In the heat of battle, each player is free to make his own decisions'.

Mike Greenaway, the rugby journalist from Durban, wrote: 'It is a top Mallett priority that individuals express flair within the framework of an intelligent pattern that embraces the latest developments in the modern game.'

Game plans would vary according to opposition, weather, injuries and so on. The players had to be good and flexible enough to adapt to the dictates of circumstances.

After the Welsh test at Wembley in 1998, when Wales had run the Springboks close, Mallett complained that he had got the planning wrong because he had not had the opportunity to study the Welsh side beforehand and that the players had taken an hour to react to the change in circumstances instead of a few minutes. Certainly the Springboks changed.

He knew the way Graham Henry, previously of Auckland and now Wales's new coach, wanted to play from the way Auckland had played, but Mallett made the mistake of doubting that Henry could do it with the Welsh side. But he did. He brought in some big backs as well as big forwards, men who could stand up in the tackle. He changed Neil Jenkins at flyhalf. He played superbly, not taking the ball up but standing back and distributing cleverly. Wales proved the value of a coach, especially one who can select well. All of this said: it is possible that the Springboks did not spend enough time analysing their opponents' play.

Mallett has also said: 'I'm a perfectionist and have always striven for perfection. I am completely passionate about the game, and if we plan something and don't stick to it, it annoys me.'

Planning is obviously needed for a match but not a hard-and-fast game plan. Apart from Mallett's general philosophy of retaining possession to score tries, there was specific planning for each match. Mallett and Solomons would meet at the start of each week to plan the week – planning for the needs of a specific match, according to the nature of the opposition and to avoid being predictable.

Mallett made it clear to his team that he was with them till the end of the 1999 World Cup. He was more concerned that they enjoy their rugby, play quickly and vary the game than he was with initial success in the full knowledge that the results would come. They came more quickly than he had anticipated.

His communication skills were also invaluable in getting the press on his side. He said at the start of the time of his appointment: 'The media made André Markgraaff's life a misery and Carel du Plessis's life a misery. I just hope they don't make mine a misery, but I 'm sure I'll handle it.'

This he did from the start with his transparent, inclusive style of management but, above all, with the team's success. As Louis de Villiers of *Rapport* said: 'At my age I wouldn't have thought it possible, but I hero-worship this man.'

He would build up good relations with the media by being open with them, expecting mutual respect between his team and the media, having both sides understand each other's needs and ensuring that there was no harbouring of grudges. It was easy for the players to resent an individual's expressed opinion of their performance or ability.

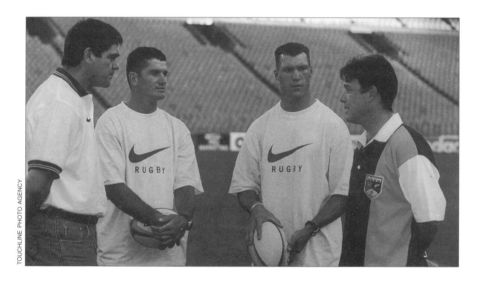

Nick Mallett with Joost van der Westhuizen and André Snyman in conversation with Darren Scott of the television programme *Boots 'n All*.

Mike Greenaway, a reporter with more insight than many, wrote: 'A rare mix of intelligence, passion and sporting prowess, Mallett has obliterated the secrecy, hidden agendas and political baggage under which Springboks traditionally struggled, freeing the players to revel in an unprecedented environment of transparency, openness and participative management.'

Mallett made himself available to the media. On tour, he made himself available for three two-hour sessions with the press – on Mondays, Thursdays and the Saturday-Sunday after matches. These would include general press conferences as well as one-on-ones, especially for radio and television. Besides that, he was available. Media people had simply to organise an interview through Alex Broun.

One form of communication which grew, and through which he was able to show the good face of Springbok rugby, serious but with a smile, was in making speeches. Mallett was increasingly in demand at dinners and other functions, and on magazine programmes on television. After the Tri-Nations in 1998 he made on average one speech a week. He did it well – articulate, amusing, patently honest. For the same reasons he was much in demand for magazine articles, appearing on cover after cover – possibly the second best-known face in South Africa after Nelson Mandela.

Dave Mallett, headmaster of Western Province Preparatory School (WPPS), had during 1998 engaged Professor Jonathan Jansen of the University of Durban Westville, an expert on outcomes-based education, to speak at his prize-giving. He was to leave Durban on the 7 am flight. He phoned Dave to tell him that he had had a puncture on the way to the airport and had missed his plane.

Dave phoned Morné du Plessis, a member of his board of governors. Morné answered in a hoarse voice and he suggested Nick.

Dave phoned Nick at quarter to ten and got him cleaning the pool at his Constantia home. At twenty past ten Nick was on stage. His brother introduced him and he gave the boys of WPPS an excellent address.

Nick Mallett has often appeared on television programmes. These have included a television documentary on the BBC, shown as part of the build-up to the South Africa-Wales test in November 1998, an appearance with Dali Tambo on his show *People of the South* in which Mallett rendered his easy-talking host virtually speechless but which Tambo seemed to enjoy thoroughly, and frequently on the Tuesday night show *Boots 'n All* on M-Net.

He shared one *Boots 'n All* show with Bobby Skinstad. It was a fun performance. At one stage Skinstad, who had frequently been interrupted by Mallett, appealed to the presenter, Darren Scott, for a fair chance to speak and drew an imaginary line between himself and his coach, who also enjoyed the moment.

Communicating well requires clear thought. So does effective selection. Nick Mallett has the sort of head which makes him, like Kitch Christie and André Markgraaff, an excellent selector. In Mallett's coaching time, a selection committee was put in place – Mickey Gerber, convener, Francois Davis and Mallett himself. Mallett has the casting vote and is the sole selector of test teams. The other two act more in an advisory capacity, a happy arrangement. All of his selections have had logic behind them.

One of his clearly stated policies from the start was not to choose players playing overseas, which annoyed men like François Pienaar and Joel Stransky, neither of whom were likely to have featured in Mallett's plans anyway. The one who would have been chosen had he still been in South Africa was Fritz van Heerden, the Western Province and Springbok lock/flank, who was a magnificent catcher of the ball at kick-offs. Mallett said: 'If guys are overseas, it's tough. I don't think you can compare a Northern Transvaal-Auckland game with Bath against Leicester. I would really like it if players stayed in South Africa to be part of the Springbok side.' In 1999 Fritz van Heeden was set to return to South Africa.

François Pienaar, the player/coach of Saracens, did not like the idea of selecting Springboks only from those playing in South Africa. In an article in the *Sunday Telegraph* before the 1997 tour, he said: 'The Springbok team has a very patchy look without overseas players.' To him it was inexperienced and Gary Teichmann was the captain 'because there was no one else around'.

These words were not prophetic as the Springboks, on that tour, posted record scores against France, Scotland and England, and Teichmann went on to play the most consecutive matches ever for a Springbok and eventually eclipsed Pienaar's own record as a Springbok captain. At the end of 1998 two foreign publications of repute, *Rugby World* in the United Kingdom and *Rugby News* in New Zealand, voted Gary Teichmann International Player of the Year for 1998, the same year that he was voted Player of the Year in South Africa.

François Pienaar almost ate his words after the magnificent victory in Paris, though he could not quite let go. He said: 'It is unfortunate that events have conspired to prevent myself from playing internationally for the last two seasons. However I take great pride in the victory over France, as it showed that the new South African team are developing into world-beaters. It is disappointing that I am not playing at such a level but yesterday was a tremendous thrill.'

On the night before the England test in 1998 Pienaar joined the Springboks at a private showing of the film *Rush Hour* by Disney's Etienne de Villiers. After it he praised Teichmann: 'If there is one man who can be singled out, it is Gary Teichmann. He handles the players in the right way and they have an outstanding relationship.'

It was clear from all of this that Mallett was heart and soul in South African rugby. He was more than a coach. 'It's not a job. It's a passion for me.'

This passion translates into many things, including determination. His concentration on the task at hand is absolute. Even more than in his father's case, his focus on the task at hand will blot out whatever is going on around him. In that, he is like his friend, André Markgraaff.

At times his passion has run over. As a club or provincial coach, he would prowl up and down the touch line, explaining vociferously what he wanted and, at times, giving the referee great chunks of his mind. As Springbok coach, greater dignity was required. The exterior self-control battled to keep the lid on the boiling tensions within.

'In France one learns to show one's emotions. You wave your arms and say what you think. South Africans are more conservative, more introverted. They don't expect their coaches to do such things. I can't change what I am, but I understand that people watch the man who coaches the Springboks. I suppose I'll have to be a bit calmer now.'

Externally he was certainly calmer and more dignified than Clive Woodward, the English coach, or Donal Lenihan, the Irish manager, or Ian McIntosh, the Natal and former Springbok coach. But it did not stop him from waking up at 5 am and worrying.

Nick Mallett is competitive. He plays table tennis as if it were the heavyweight championship of the world. He will play a hand of bridge as if he were deciding the fate of nations. Losing is not a joy.

On one occasion he was playing bridge with his mother at home in an event with four tables. She made a mistake which cost them a contract. He told her where she had gone wrong and said: 'I've never known you make such an elementary mistake. It's so unlike you.' They moved from table to table and Nick kept up his explanation of what should have happened and his astonishment that it had happened. Some twenty minutes later Vivienne said: 'I've had quite enough of that hand, thank you. You've made your point.'

He and Tim Brukman were playing tennis singles at Knysna, where the Brukmans had a holiday home on Leisure Isle. It was, inevitably, another McEnroe-Connors affair, rather than a social knock-about. The two were roughly even in ability and this time Tim won. The winning shot came when Tim lobbed a Mallett smash over his head. It landed a centimetre inside the base line with Mallett chasing after it in such desperation that he crashed into the back fence.

Afterwards, as they sat down, Mallett's mood was black. Tim said: 'You could be more gracious in defeat.'

Mallett replied: 'I'm a bad loser and proud of it. The only good loser is the one who's used to losing.'

Nick Pagden, a close friend from St Andrew's and UCT days, first met Nick when they were prep school boys. Mallett's parents were staying with Griff Mullins at St Andrew's Prep, where Pagden was at school. Pagden and a friend were playing gaining ground, a kicking game, on the field when Mallett arrived with Tizzy behind him. He announced 'My sister and I would like to challenge you two to a game of gaining ground.' Pagden asked if Tizzy was good enough. Mallett gave the assurance and suddenly placid gaining ground became a test match dominated by the biggest boot of the lot – Tizzy's.

Naturally this competitiveness affected his coaching. He has theories about coaching, but they are practical ones aimed at victory. After all, players and fans prefer victory to anything else. He said: 'Rugby is a practical game dealing with tangible problems, not about idealistic notions of how one wishes it to be played.'

Head and heart working together came out best in his caring commitment to his team.

LEADERSHIP

Nick Mallett's first job as coach was to choose the team to tour Italy, France (two tests), Scotland and England at the end of 1997. He brought back Adrian Garvey, whom Carel du Plessis had left out. He brought in Krynauw Otto, the big, mobile Northern Transvaal lock, who had been a Dirt Tracker on the 1996 tour, and who was to develop into one of the best locks in the world.

Both of these players, neglected by Du Plessis, represented the mobile kind of tight forward that Mallett sought, the man who, above all, could tackle. With a 'tight five' of the mobility of Os du Randt, James Dalton, Adrian Garvey, Mark Andrews and Krynauw Otto, Mallett could take on anybody. At the end of 1997 he already believed that Andrews and Otto were the best lock combination in world rugby.

In 1998 he chose two athletic locks again, Johnny Trytsman and Selborne Boome, both of whom had played loose-forward at a high level.

Mallett brought in the veteran Dick Muir, who had intended retiring in 1997 but had got a new lease on life when his old friend Harry Viljoen brought him to Western Province as the captain of the team – a successful captain, too, for his team won the Currie Cup. Muir's speed was gone, but not his courage or his ability to communicate. At inside centre he was able to marshal the backs and bring out the best in Henry Honiball at flyhalf. Honiball, too, became a fixture in the Mallett teams after Carel had discarded him for Jannie de Beer, the Free Stater with the big boot.

A blow, especially in the absence of Ruben Kruger through injury, was the injury to Corné Krige in the 1997 Currie Cup final, which ruled out the tall flank with the deadly tackle and remarkable work-rate. But Krige came back to play in the 1998 Currie Cup final, survived and was a successful tourist with the 1998 Springboks, only to suffer further injury early in 1999.

Unlike the announcement in 1996, this 1997 touring team was announced in orderly fashion and without controversy. It was Mallett's first selection and it made sense:

THE TOURING TEAM: Justin Swart, Thinus Delport, Percy Montgomery, MacNiel Hendricks, Pieter Rossouw, James Small, Breyton Paulse, Dick Muir, André Snyman, Joe Gillingham, Franco Smith, Boeta Wessels, Henry Honiball, Jannie de Beer, Joost van der Westhuizen, Werner Swanepoel, Dan van Zyl, Gary Teichmann (captain), Andrew Aitken, Johan Erasmus, André Venter, Warren Brosnihan, Bobby Skinstad, Philip Smit, Braam Els, Wium Basson, Krynauw Otto, Mark Andrews, Adrian Garvey, Dawie Theron, Toks van der Linde, Ollie le Roux, Willie Meyer, James Dalton, Naka Drotské, Dale Santon.

It was a successful team. Nick Mallett was uncharacteristically self-deprecating when he spoke about his coaching and the plaudits that echoed about his team's success:

MALLETT FAMILY COLLECTION

ABOVE The Saint Claude team. David Mallett is third from the right in the back row. Nick is second right.
RIGHT A Springbok in Paris. Nick Mallett about to pack down in the AC Boulogne-Billancourt scrum.

SPORT FOR AFRICA

MALLETT FAMILY COLLECTION

MALLETT FAMILY COLLECTION

Top Nick with daughter Kate.
Above The family: Kate, Doug, Nick and Jane.
Opposite Nick and Doug stretch against the garage of their Constantia home.

PREVIOUS PAGES The Springboks go through their stretching routine in 1998, while Mallett casts a sombre eye. Corné Krige is immediately in front of him and Naka Drotské facing on the right.
OPPOSITE Touch rugby with Nick Mallett about to pounce on Krynauw Otto.
RIGHT Part of the management team – Nick Mallett, Alan Solomons and Peter de Villiers.
BELOW Before the Welsh test in 1998, Mallett hands Mark Andrews a special jersey for his 50th test.

SARFU COLLECTION

TERTIUS PICKARD/TOUCHLINE PHOTO AGENCY

TOP Gary Teichmann, Arthob Petersen and Nick Mallett meet President Mandela. ABOVE Jake White, the Springbok's technical adviser, with ball in hand.

RIGHT Doc Frans Verster in action.

BELOW Lisa Bon, SARFU's public relations manager, provides Nick Mallett with off-the-field back up. She is seen here with, from left, Tobie Titus (member SARFU Executive Committee), Sas Bailey (SARFU General Manager, Development), Johannes Conradie (Under 21 'Baby Bok'), Mr Lottering ('Baby Bok's' teacher), Rian Oberholzer (SARFU CEO), Howard Wilson ('Baby Bok's' teacher), Germaine Brinkhuys (Under 21 'Baby Bok') and Cliffie Booysen (SARFU Youth Manager).

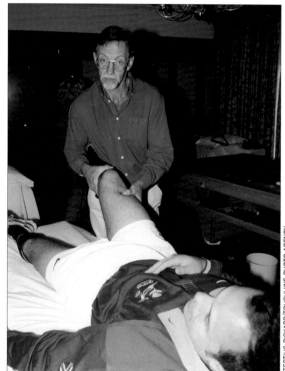

TERTIUS PICKARD/TOUCHLINE PHOTO AGENCY

SARFU COLLECTION

TERTIUS PICKARD/TOUCHLINE PHOTO AGENCY

GERHARD STEENKAMP FOTOGRAFIE

TERTIUS PICKARD/TOUCHLINE PHOTO AGENCY

TERTIUS PICKARD/TOUCHLINE PHOTO AGENCY

OPPOSITE TOP Rassie Erasmus bursts past Diego Dominguez in Bologna, Italy.

OPPOSITE BOTTOM Stefan Terblanche knows it's a try, and Gary Teichmann is claiming it. The All Blacks are looking up in horror. Peter Marshall confirmed it was a try and South Africa won an astonishing victory in Durban!

ABOVE MacNiel Hendricks on his way to scoring a try against Wales, to the delight of Naka Drotské.

LEFT The South African diaspora gave the Springboks fervent support wherever they played overseas, and the Springboks in turn gave their supporters much to be proud of.

ABOVE The Springboks do their lap of honour in their farewell to the Parc des Princes in 1998.
LEFT Captain Courageous, Gary Teichmann ploughs into England at Newlands, 1998!
OPPOSITE TOP Bobby Skinstad on one of his devastating runs against Ireland at Lansdowne Road in 1998.
OPPOSITE BOTTOM Joost van der Westhuizen low and sniping against England at Newlands in 1998.

TERTIUS PICKARD/TOUCHLINE PHOTO AGENCY

TERTIUS PICKARD/TOUCHLINE PHOTO AGENCY

TERTIUS PICKARD/TOUCHLINE PHOTO AGENCY

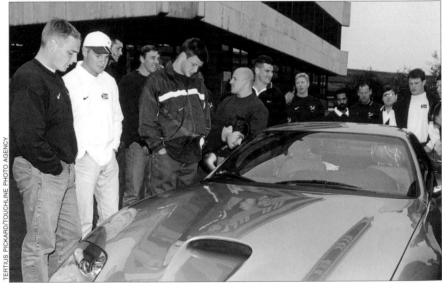

TERTIUS PICKARD/TOUCHLINE PHOTO AGENCY

JAN HAMMAN/*DIE BEELD*

TERTIUS PICKARD/TOUCHLINE PHOTO AGENCY

OPPOSITE TOP The Springboks on their 1998 visit to Robben Island. OPPOSITE BOTTOM Now that's a car! The Springboks at the Ferrari factory in 1997. ABOVE Golf at Mt Edgecombe when the Springboks and the All Blacks met on the day after the Durban test in 1998. Watching the ball go are Gary Teichmann, Henry Honiball and Nick Mallett. LEFT André Vos plays barber to Robbie Kempson on the 1998 tour. FOLLOWING PAGE Intense, determined, confident – Mallett the coach.

'If you do well, people think you are a fantastic coach, but all you do is get a couple of guys you can trust and you get some organisation.'

To earn trust, the organisation needed to be player-centred. Players did not change from generation to generation. They wanted the opportunity to win well for the country or whatever team they were playing for. He saw it as management's duty to enable them to do just that. And he said: 'To help them you should ask their opinion.'

He wanted the players to buy into the tour and the running of the tour. He wanted the players to take responsibility for discipline, use of alcohol, rooming lists, punctuality, manners and co-operation with the sponsors and the media.

Mallett said of the Springboks: 'They want to be more professional, more polite, to mix with people after the game, to sell their country, to sell themselves, to sell rugby on the field, sell everything.' He wanted to end the rude, arrogant image of the Springboks. 'I would like to change the perception that South African rugby is played by guys from the highveld who just grunt. I want to put a stop to people thinking of us as brutal.'

He started with a strategic planning workshop, run by Tim Southey, a disciple of Colin Hall of Wooltru and the human resources manager of Norwich Life, the generous sponsors of Western Province rugby.

In 1997 Harry Viljoen became the Western Province coach after the proud union had experienced an unsatisfactory year. A millionaire businessman and a creative rugby coach, Viljoen was also associated with Norwich Life. He had heard about Southey's work and asked his help. Viljoen wanted to rid himself and the rest of his coaching team of management baggage, such as contracts, discipline issues, clothes and travelling, so that he could focus on the Western Province team, to turn them around so that they could reach the final of the Currie Cup. He wanted the organisation of the team to be transformed. Western Province won the cup in 1997.

Alan Solomons was Viljoen's assistant and saw the value in what Southey was doing. When Nick Mallett became the Springbok coach, Solomons told him about Southey, whom Mallett subsequently met.

Tim Southey was only too keen to get involved. He recalled: 'At the time the players were at an all-time low. It was at the end of a long season and the Springboks had lost several games on the trot. Nick had less than a week to mobilise support and get the guys ready before they flew off to Europe.'

The first thing Southey required of Mallett was a careful articulation of his vision and goals. It was not enough to be simplistic and say that he wanted the Springboks to thrash everybody. It had to be better than that. Southey believed that what Mallett came up with was brilliant, clear and also philosophical: the establishment of a winning culture on and off the field, and to put pride back into South African rugby.

That was what Mallett wanted. The next thing was to establish how it was to be done. The best way to achieve their goal was to empower the players and allow them the space to achieve their goal. They needed to buy into the scheme heart and soul, and to do so they needed to make the important decisions, leaving Nick and his coaches free to concentrate on the rugby.

Southey identified the need for the players to take ownership of what happened on the field, off the field, at practice, in contact with the media and in their accountability to those who watched them play, whom they were to see as their customers. They needed to be aware that professionalism was not just about being paid but was about taking responsibility.

Southey was anxious. 'I had done this with a lot of executives and once with the Western Province rugby team, but I was nervous. I wondered whether they would say: "What is all this mumbo jumbo?" But they took to it like ducks to water. Their sense of maturity and accountability was unbelievable.'

Time was of the essence as the team would be leaving in a matter of days for Europe, but they set aside two days, broken by a little practice, for strategic workshops on 27 and 28 October 1997. These were aimed at getting a clear focus on their goals and then producing a code of conduct that every one of them would subscribe to.

The players would talk. They would bring out what had been frustrations and obstacles in the past while Mallett sat quietly and listened without interrupting. Then the 36 players were divided into six groups of six each, each with a leader who would be a monitor for his group for the rest of the tour. The leaders were Gary Teichmann, Joost van der Westhuizen, Dick Muir, Andrew Aitken, Mark Andrews and James Small. Of them, Muir and Aitken had not yet played a test, but they were both experienced, intelligent men with proven leadership qualities. James Small, often the rebel, revelled in it. 'The trust the management is putting in me makes me more responsible. For the first time since 1992, the coach is part of the team, and that is vital.' Small would break records and, sadly, also play his last test on the tour.

Nick Mallett kicked off the session with his overview, quietly at first, then with the full force of Mallett passion. Tim Southey acted as facilitator and then the players got stuck into four particular issues: an analysis of the team's strengths and weaknesses; the spirit (*gees*) in the team; a professional code of conduct on and off the field; and discipline and standards. It was a management style better suited to the new generation of rugby player. This was real and practical transformation.

In analysing their strengths and weaknesses they looked at what was working for them, what was working against them and what they should do differently. On the matter of team spirit they looked at what built and what broke down team spirit and how they should develop team spirit to its best. This got down to issues such as entertainment and rooming lists. The professional code of conduct, on and off the field, looked at things such as manners, socialising, use of alcohol, dress and mixing with opponents. The players established their disciplinary committee (Small, Van der Westhuizen and Andrews) and their ways of dealing with infractions of the disciplinary code, with the proviso that serious infractions would be matters for the management team.

The players got stuck into their workshop and produced a three-page code of conduct for the tour. Having drawn the document up themselves, there could be little debate about it afterwards. Having signed it, they could hardly wriggle out of it.

Nick Mallett was delighted with what they produced. 'It is fantastic. They came up with the sort of thing I hoped for.'

Mallett would also say that tolerance of one another became an important by-product of the process. He wanted to get rid of the kontiki, the players' meeting which would include initiation of new players once they had made an appearance on the field. The players wanted to keep it. It stayed. Mallett had not been one for saying prayers around rugby matches. But the players wanted to continue to do so and so the custom stayed. The prayers were not about victory but for protection and in gratitude for the opportunities of fellowship and expression of talents.

Mallett believed that teams needed tolerance of each other, as did he. What he wanted most was to bring out the rugby ability in each player. Everything else was a means to the end of getting the best out of them.

The groups became useful for competition within the team for all sorts of things – from singing training to skill drills. It was just what Mallett would do playing on the beach with his children and friends. There would be a competition in it, such as seeing who could hit a rock five times.

Mallett said of his management style: 'I'm more consultative than the other coaches have been. I believe the guys are adults and should show self-responsibility.'

When the Springboks were in France, Joost van der Westhuizen said: 'Nick handles the guys like adults. He's helped the players to grow up and perform in their own way. The players have an input into everything that is going on while we are on tour and are more relaxed because of that.' James Dalton said: 'Nick's openness and approachability are the keys to his success.' And then he added: 'He may seem to be cheerful, but he can be tough as well. Now and again rugby players need to be spoken to in a harsh manner and we accept that if we don't perform.'

It is a constant theme from the players. Mark Andrews had not wanted to tour, a not uncommon phenomenon in the age when there was a tour every year and the rugby seasons were getting longer and longer. Andrews also capitulated to the Mallett style and admitted: 'He's just made sure we're a happy team.'

Adrian Garvey, discarded by Carel du Plessis but back again under Mallett, said near the end of the tour: 'Nick has made us feel we have much greater control over our own destiny than before, and it has contributed to a very happy squad which has gone out in each match to vindicate his faith.'

On their return to South Africa after the 1997 tour, Gary Teichmann said: 'When we convened in Johannesburg to prepare for the tour, there were a lot of long faces. For most of us it had been a long, disappointing season. I know I couldn't face touring. But Nick was so positive that, by the time we left for Italy, we resolved at a players' meeting that we would not be happy with anything less than five victories in our five test matches.'

The *Financial Mail* on 2 October 1998 carried an article on the Springboks, written by Stuart Rutherford. The article was headed: 'MORE TO THE GAME THAN MEETS THE EYE', with a subheading 'What the Boks can teach business'.

In the article Mallett is quoted as saying that one of the essential elements of the team's success was the fact that they were working to a code of conduct, which amounted to a business plan.

He highlighted from the code of conduct the total commitment of the players to each other and to the squad, no provincialism, no excuses or complaining, and singing the anthem with pride.

Tim Southey summed it up: 'In most organisations, less than 50 per cent of the potential human energy is utilised, whereas in this particular team you could almost say that the maximum physical and mental energy is being utilised.'

He believed that the success was a result of the synergy of Mallett's leadership, the players' readiness for change and Gary Teichmann's support for Nick's philosophy. There is no doubt that a large part of that leadership was Mallett's driving honesty. The players were treated with forthright directness and knew where they stood. They also knew that their coach would not tolerate selfishness, backbiting and dishonesty. The Springboks broke out of the cocoon of introspection and became an honest and colourful team. The difficulty with being honest with players is knowing when to be honest. There is a time to speak and a time to be quiet, a time to criticise and a time to encourage, a time to be tough and a time to let go. Part of Mallett's success has been his timing in the treatment of his players. Jake White believes that Mallett's greatest attribute is his ability to press the right button in his dealings with players and get them motivated, from the youngest to the most senior. The shining example of what he can get out of a player has been Krynauw Otto.

David Williams of the *Financial Mail* had a wider view. He wrote: 'The most impressive thing about Nick Mallett is not his coaching credentials or capacity for leadership, but his sense of the big picture.' The 'big picture' was rugby's potential for making a good, progressive contribution to the new South Africa.

Nick Mallett talks incisively to his team at half-time. This is the time to be precise and determined.

DUIF DU TOIT/TOUCHLINE PHOTO AGENCY

1997 TOUR

On 30 October 1997 Jane flew up to join Nick in Johannesburg. It was his birthday and the two skipped off quietly to celebrate at a fish restaurant at Sandton Square. They soon learnt that anonymity was impossible but that the position had its advantages as the restaurateur produced a complimentary bottle of excellent wine.

Then it was off to Europe – yet again. It was the third end-of-year tour aimed at saving the reputation of Springbok rugby. After Ian McIntosh's unhappy dismissal in 1994, Kitch Christie took the team to the United Kingdom – a 'hospital job', as he called it. He took them again at the end of 1995 but then they were the holders of the World Cup. After the tatters and dramas of 1996, the Springboks went to Argentina and Europe to recuperate – successfully as it turned out. Now they were on their way again – the third hospital job.

ITALY

The tour started with a test in ancient Bologna in Northern Italy, the heartland of Italian rugby. The test was a vital one for Nick Mallett – his first as Springbok coach – and although it seemed a comparatively gentle start, Italy were not pushovers. In the rest of their 1997-98 season, Italian rugby enjoyed much success and improved its standing in the rugby world, smoothing the way for Italy's admission to competition with England, Scotland, Ireland, Wales and France in the new Six Nations Championship in the year 2000.

The Springboks recorded a convincing victory over the Azzurri on 8 November 1997. Interestingly, the Italians scored three tries. In the next test France scored three tries. But no other team in the next 14 tests scored three tries against Mallett's Springboks, not even the powerful All Blacks or the creative Wallabies. But in Bologna the Springboks scored nine tries, giving Europe a wake-up call. They won 62-31. The Springboks were back in town! Afterwards, Gary Teichmann said: 'We feel much the same as we did this time last year, and hopefully we will be back with similar results.' Mallett said: 'The tour will be a happy one, if we keep winning.'

Ominously, they were penalised numerous times. The Argentinian referee did to them in Bologna what he had done previously in Rosario and Lille and would do to the Under 21 side when they played a curtain-raiser to the England test in 1998.

Disaster was not far off. The Springboks met the French Barbarians in Biarritz. The Springbok front row was battling against a front row made up of Pierre de Villiers, a powerful young South African at tight-head, Vincent Moscato and Jean-Jacques Crenca. Just on half-time, big Toks van der Linde, playing loose-head, charged into a ruck, boots first. A boot found the face of David Dantiacq, who was prone on the ground. The referee, Joel Dumé of France, sent the prop off, as he was well entitled to do. The Springboks kept on playing badly and lost 40-22, making the French Barbarians one of the few non-test sides in the world to have beaten the Springboks three times. Losing the big prop was, of course, a blow.

There was no protection for Toks van der Linde from his team-mates. The players' committee discussed the matter and fined their team-mate. Toks van der Linde returned home, suspended for 60 days. Mallett spoke of 'testosterone charged aggression'. He said: 'There's no place for putting your feet on a man who's on the ground.' He also said: 'South African rugby is no more dirty or violent than any other. I've played here in France for nine years and that was far more violent and far dirtier than anything I've had to put up with in South Africa.'

It was an expensive experience for Toks. Early in the next season, he incurred further displeasure and an early dispatch from New Zealand when he hurled a racial insult at a woman in a Christchurch bar. Again it cost him dearly. Again he was sent home. At the end of 1998 he was chosen for the Springboks and toured well through Scotland and Ireland, probably unlucky not to have a place in the test team. But before he could tour he had a chat with Mallett who said that he would choose the big prop provided he publicly apologised for his action. Mallett went to see Steve Tshwete, the Minister of Sport, who gave him the go-ahead to pick him.

In 1997 Mallett also chastised Wium Basson, the young Northern Transvaal lock, who had a disappointing tour. Mallett was not going to allow or tolerate ill discipline. Basson did not tour in 1998.

Having told his team not to retaliate was one thing. What to do if they did was another. What to do if the opposition took advantage of their pacifism was yet another.

In 1998 Ireland played South Africa, and were violent. The violence was led by their captain Paddy Johns, who tackled Gaffie du Toit late in the first minute, and Keith Wood, their combative hooker, who laid into Gary Teichmann. The Springboks did not retaliate.

The second test was at Loftus Versfeld. Mallett spoke to the Springboks and warned them, but he knew his words were falling on deaf ears. The Springboks were going to get stuck in. Keith Wood left the field a battered man, much to the Springboks' delight. It was an unsavoury match.

Mallett believed that Wood should have been sent off during the Bloemfontein test for his attack on Gary Teichmann. He said: 'I thought that was a deliberate act of aggression, and I believe that if I had cited him he would have been out for six weeks.' But after the Loftus Versfeld match, where the most guilty player appeared to be Joost van der Westhuizen, there were no citings. Mallett said: 'A number of incidents were dealt with by the referee and touch judges and, after talking to the Irish management, we decided not to cite anyone, though we are very disappointed by the lack of discipline shown by the players.'

He further said that he had believed the Springbok pack was not aggressive enough in the first test; he wanted 'controlled aggression'. And this is what he got in the second test. Before the Ireland test in Dublin at the end of 1998, there was much talk of vengeance.

After all, during the speeches in Pretoria Paddy Johns, an unconciliatory captain, had told Gary Teichmann that the Irish would be waiting for the Springboks in Dublin. Teichmann expressed his unwillingness to stand back.

As it turned out, the Dublin match in 1998 was cantankerous but not as uncontrolled as the Loftus Versfeld match had been. Keith Wood – again – was given a yellow card for foul play, when he went into Joost van der Westhuizen's back with his knees while the scrumhalf was lying prone on the ground. One wondered what Wood needed to do to get sent off. On the other hand he did not finish this match either as he limped off injured.

On their end-of-year tour in 1998 the Springboks met the Glasgow Caledonians. In that match Jason White of the Caledonians stamped on the face of Braam van Straaten as the chunky flyhalf lay pinned at the bottom of a ruck. The referee seemed in a perfect position to see it but did not react, instead penalising the Springboks. The touch judges did not act either, though they had earlier flagged Willie Meyer and Corné Krige. Braam van Straaten, despite the protection of close headgear, left the field with a gashed face. This time, Mallett cited.

It was the first time the Springboks had ever cited opponents, believing that such actions lead too often to tit-for-tat situations. As it was, Allan Hosie, the former international referee and at the time the chairman of the Four Home Unions, had been the match commissioner at that match in Glasgow, and chaired the hearing into Jason White's action at a meeting in Glasgow. The Springboks, at their own expense, flew Rob van der Valk to attend. Hosie afterwards expressed his dissatisfaction with comments on the hearing before it had happened. Jason White had his father, a player and a lawyer along. Rob van der Valk presented a terse case: 'unlawful use of the boot'. There was video evidence.

White was found guilty and suspended for 116 days, virtually the rest of the season. The sentence was actually 120 days but four had been served in the run-up to the hearing. He appealed. The appeal was rejected. The Scottish Rugby Union did not want Scottish mothers seeing their children suffer similarly.

When the Springboks played against Wales later in the year, they were assaulted once more. This time they did not retaliate, but Gary Teichmann in particular took a severe blow. There was no action taken against Scott Quinnell who flattened him with a neck tackle before Teichmann had even got the ball. The Springbok captain again suffered a neck injury, again had tingling down his arm. The British press did not seem to mind Quinnell's action and instead criticised Teichmann's performance in a condescending way. Some people looked to Mallett to cite again to protect his player who was forbidden to retaliate. He did not do so.

In 1997 Toks van der Linde had no leniency and went home to pay his penance, while the team moved on to France, to Lyon, a part of the world Mallett knew well. Lyon is a grand city at the confluence of the Rhône and the Saone rivers, with their powerful Alpine waters. It is really a soccer city and once again the match was played on a soccer ground, Stade de Gerland, revamped for the soccer World Cup. It was too big for the 25 000 people who arrived to watch rugby on 15 November 1997, but what a wonderful test match it was!

FRANCE

Justin Swart had played well against Italy but strained a hamstring. When Swart was ruled out of the second test of the tour, the first against France, Mallett surprised many people by moving Percy Montgomery to fullback. HO de Villiers, the famous Springbok fullback of the late 1960s, one of the first attacking fullbacks, had helped coach SACS when Montgomery was in the school's first XV and had suggested to Mallett that he move Montgomery to the position he knew best – fullback. The eager young player had played more matches at centre for South Africa than for any other team. He had played wing. His club had used him as a flyhalf, but Monty really yearned to play fullback.

The change of position was an eye-opener! Percy Montgomery was brilliant. Soon people were comparing him favourably to All Black Christian Cullen, with his explosive, daring running.

Playing France in France is not easy. The 1996 Springboks had won both tests on French soil, the second by a point in Paris. But such a victory was a feat which the 1992 Springbok visitors did not manage, the Wallabies have not managed it on four trips to France (the last in 1993) and the All Blacks did not manage in 1995. The last touring team to win a series in France was the All Blacks in 1990, the year Romania, for the only time, beat France in France.

In 1997 the Springboks came to a stronger-looking French team than the one of the year before.

At the Stade de Gerland in Lyon, France kicked deep. Werner Swanepoel caught the ball and slung a pass inside to Percy Montgomery. The fullback ran, and suddenly the Springboks were rampant. André Snyman cut through and scored. With eleven minutes to go, the Springboks led 36-15, but the proud French came back, spearheaded by Olivier Merle, the massive lock who looked as if he could have stormed the Bastille single-handedly.

At the final whistle the Springboks clung desperately to the lead and were ahead 36-32 and a great test match came to an end.

Philippe Saint-André, the French captain, said afterwards: 'We were surprised by the intensity of the game early on. We are just not used to playing at that sort of level.'

There was great praise for Mallett's team. The *Cape Argus* headline ran: 'MALLETT'S MARVELS'.

Mallett said: 'I'm pleased, and proud of the way we played.' He was learning the art of understatement. He also knew what every sportsman eventually learns – to win humbly, for defeat is only a match away.

Gary Teichmann's comment was also cautiously pleased: 'They were lions today but we held our nerve – just.'

The next match was poor. Played in Toulon, France A beat the mid-week Springboks 21-7. The Springboks again failed to come up to scratch, which suggested that the Springbok cream was, as many overseas commentators insisted, thin. That tune changed somewhat in 1998, but it looked valid then.

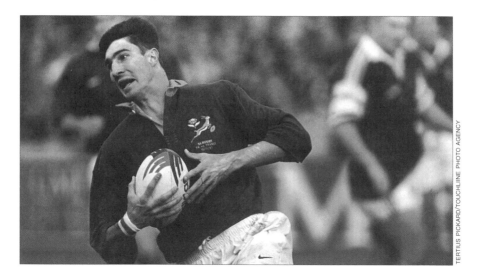

TERTIUS PICKARD/TOUCHLINE PHOTO AGENCY

Pieter Rossouw scoring one of his four magnificent tries against France in 1997.

On the Springboks went to Parc des Princes, but with trepidation. The year before, they had won there but by only a point, when Ruben Kruger charged down a dropped goal attempt in the dying seconds of the match.

For this match the French picked Olivier Merle in their starting line-up, hoping that the robust forward would last the pace, for his fitness was suspect.

Parc des Princes is a ground of great atmosphere, a place of noisy, fervent participation. This time there was even greater reason for fervour. It was to be the last test at Parc des Princes before the French moved on to the big new Stade de France in the northern suburbs. It was a special occasion and the French produced many great players to parade beforehand, including JPR Williams, who said: 'This stadium is second to none in the whole world.'

At the end of the match the French crowd, appreciative of the rugby played, cheered as the Springboks did a lap of honour. They cheered after jeering their own team off the field. For the Springboks had played rugby from heaven to score a record 52-10, seven tries to one, victory over France. It broke the South African record of 38-5, posted in Bordeaux in 1913. It was the highest score ever against France, and scoring seven tries was also a record against France. Pieter Rossouw became the first player to score four tries in a test at Parc des Princes. In doing so he equalled Chester Williams's Springbok record set against Western Samoa in 1995. In 1998 Stefan Terblanche would become the third Springbok to perform this feat, in his case on début.

It was a day of Springbok glory as 56 000 Frenchmen changed their chant from *Allez Bleus* to *Les Boks, Les Boks*. But by half-time the Boks had already endeared themselves

The marvellous Springboks who broke records against France in Lyon in 1997.

to the home crowd. At half-time the Springbok bench and the French bench were keeping warm and playing touch rugby, each in a separate part of the field. Dan van Zyl, the chirpy Springbok scrumhalf, gestured to the French to join the Springboks. They played touch rugby against each other. Dan van Zyl got space and ran through for a perky try, and the Parc des Princes crowd cheered.

The greatest moment of the test was Henry Honiball's first try in international rugby. Deep in the Springbok 22, Werner Swanepoel passed to Dick Muir, the veteran centre. Muir passed to Percy Montgomery. Montgomery passed to Jannie de Beer who passed to André Snyman who passed to Henry Honiball who wheeled around in disbelief before plunging over for a try, his first in a test match.

It was a try to equal in quality the famous French try at Eden Park in 1994 when the French clinched the series against the All Blacks. Mallett was praised.

André Markgraaff said: 'I take my hat off to Nick Mallett.'

Harry Viljoen said: 'It's clear the Boks are loving the way they are playing.'

Dan Retief said: 'Mallett and his team have been utterly professional in their preparation but, most of all, the empathetic coach has created a culture in which players are permitted to express their talents. Confidence could be Mallett's middle name, but the positive attitude he has engendered would be nothing had he not also instilled a style of play aimed utterly at scoring tries.'

'The win in Paris will always be something special,' Mallett said. 'No team has ever done what we did. The players know this. They have had the celebratory beers and know that the work continues.' Mallett's team deserved those beers. They had come off a humiliating season and here they were riding the crest of the wave, hailed by the French as a great team.

TO ENGLAND AND SCOTLAND

The British saw it differently, and the Springboks went across the Channel to a quiet welcome. English rugby was focused on visitors all right – but on the All Blacks. A year later things would be different at Heathrow, and in the whole of Britain. Then, when the Springboks came into the airport concourse, *Hier Kom die Bokke* was being played and the British press was full of them. They would rise to greatness in 1998.

The intense British interest in the All Blacks annoyed Mallett. The Springboks and the Wallabies were being ignored.

At one press conference, a reporter asked Mallett if he thought the Springboks were in the same class as the All Blacks.

Mallett's reply was exasperated: 'What is it with you people? You have an obsessive love affair with the All Blacks. I can assure you that the Springboks are back – whether you care to notice or not. We've been in this country a week and there has been hardly a mention of our remarkable 50-point victory over France in Paris, but there are pages and pages of All Black worshipping. I cannot say how good we are compared to them, because we haven't played them or Australia. But don't you think we're due a line or two?'

In the end, the Springboks had the best test record on their end-of the-year tour.

	P	W	D	L	Pf	Pa	Tf	Ta
South Africa	5	5	0	0	247	94	35	9
New Zealand	4	3	1	0	156	56	17	7
Australia	2	1	1	0	52	23	7	1

Interestingly, after the Paris test, André Markgraaff, the most astute of rugby men, was noticing a sea change in rugby standings. He said: 'New Zealand are playing comfort-zone rugby. We are playing the more adventurous and positive game.' Perhaps he foresaw the changes due in 1998.

In the midst of the euphoria that followed the Paris victory, Nick Mallett said: 'To beat England we will have to play well.'

The way the Twickenham test kicked off it would seem that his prophecy would come true as England raced to an 11-0 lead and the crowd were singing sweetly to urge the chariot to swing low. But there was an air of unreality about it all. England were simply not going to win.

Mallett had often urged his players to be patient. Play correctly, don't panic and victory will come.

In the end the Springboks won 28-11, England's biggest defeat at Twickenham.

In the *Sunday Telegraph* Paul Ackford, the England lock turned journalist, wrote: 'Nick Mallett has changed the Springboks from the miserable, one-dimensional bunch the Lions faced this summer. Then the Springboks played a very limited game based around (sic) the driving play of massive forwards. Yesterday, the width of their game was remarkable and so was their willingness and ability to run the ball at England from all areas. The backline is light years away from the predictable, programmed group who struggled under Carel du Plessis, Mallett's predecessor.'

Not everybody was as generous. David Hands of *The Sunday Times* said: 'The England coach had suggested that South Africa had put their best 15 players out, whereas England were without two Lions amongst the backs – the injured Guscott and Underwood – Phil de Glanville, also injured and Martin Johnson due to suspension.' (Johnson had been suspended for a week for violence against Justin Marshall in the Manchester test between England and New Zealand.)

In fact, South Africa were without players of the calibre of André Joubert, Japie Mulder, Ruben Kruger and Joost van der Westhuizen.

Clive Woodward, the lively England coach, was more gracious when he spoke about the Springboks. 'They're such a happy bunch. They look excited to be playing for their country. Against England, you couldn't help noticing the pride they have in wearing the green and gold.'

Surprisingly, England's manners on the field rather let them down. To start, Richard Cockerill, a bantam cock of a hooker, circled the Springbok forwards as they huddled

André Venter and Adrian Garvey pose before the Arc de Triomphe in Paris, 1997.

together before the kick-off to tell them all sorts of rude things that would happen to their rude selves. Worse for England was the yellow card for Danny Grewcock for punching and the penalty which was reversed when Garath Archer punched.

And so it was on to Scotland, the willing, enthusiastic, amateur Scots. The Springboks were riding the crest of the wave.

The Springboks met Scotland at Murrayfield. Before the game, the anthems were being sung, the Boks singing theirs with passion. Then came *Flower of Scotland*, rugby's most popular national song. There was big Mark Andrews singing along with the Scots, a happy glint in his eye! Possibly a unique situation.

In 1951 the Springboks had thrashed the Scots – 44-0, scoring nine tries. It was a huge setback for Scottish rugby. They lost their next 13 matches and did not win another test till 1954.

In 1997 the Springboks won 68-10, Scotland's biggest defeat ever. In the process James Small broke Danie Gerber's test record for tries scored by a Springbok, thanks to Percy Montgomery.

Montgomery was the star of the match as he raced all over Murrayfield. He broke, headed for the line and with nobody in front of him and with a matter of a metre or so to go, threw Small a perfect pass so that he could break the South African record. In the process Montgomery deprived himself of a South African record. He scored 26 points that afternoon, two short of Gavin Johnson's record in a test. But Monty's turn would come: against Wales at Loftus Versfeld in 1998, when he scored 31 points.

Although it has a capacity of 67 500, only 30 000 came to Murrayfield that day. The Springboks had just not fired the British imagination the way the All Blacks had done. It would be different a year later when the Springboks were recognised as the best team in the world.

Tour Summary:

	P	W	D	L	Pf	Pa	Tf	Ta
Tests:	5	5	0	0	247	94	35	9
Mid-week:	2	0	0	2	29	61	5	7
Total:	7	5	0	2	276	155	40	6

Mark Andrews rises up above the Newlands mud to win a line-out in the 1998 England test.

GLORY IN 1998

Trumpets of confidence heralded 1998. The Springboks were back on track. They, the All Blacks and the Wallabies had all been in Europe at the end of 1997, and the Springboks had looked the best.

Their first meeting in 1998 would be in the Super 12, a competition which kicked off the 1998 season. In this five teams from New Zealand, four from South Africa and three from Australia take part. South Africa had, for the first time, introduced regional teams, made up of players from three or four provinces, and there was confidence that they would be stronger than teams from individual provinces.

Harry Viljoen, coach of the Western Province team which had won the 1997 Currie Cup, was coaching the Western Stormers, a conglomeration of Western Province, Boland and South Western Districts. Ian McIntosh had charge of the Coastal Sharks with Natal, Border and Eastern Province, a wobbly alliance as Natal kicked out to secure their naming rights and sponsorships. The Northern Bulls comprised Northern Transvaal, Mpumalanga, North West and Northern Free State, and their coach was Eugene van Wyk. But the team to take South Africa to the top of the Super 12 table, was the Golden Cats – the Gauteng Lions, as the Golden Lions were for a while, the Free State and Griqualand West. There would be Springboks everywhere.

The Super 12 was going to be great!

But the Super 12 was an almost complete disaster for South Africa. The Golden Cats, Northern Bulls and Western Stormers were poor beyond nightmare. These three South African teams were amongst the last four teams in the Super 12, while New Zealand had three teams – Auckland Blues, Canterbury Crusaders and Otago Highlanders – in the top four. The Coastal Sharks fared best of South Africa's teams and ended third, unlucky not to merit a home final and a fair chance of playing in the final. The final was an all-New Zealand affair with Canterbury Crusaders beating the mighty Auckland Blues.

At the end of the tournament, Harry Viljoen stalked out of the Stormers and Western Province, leaving behind him shell-shocked players, especially Percy Montgomery, Pieter Rossouw and Justin Swart. But the Province team managed to pick itself up and made the 1998 Currie Cup final with a succession of big wins. The Gauteng Lions became the Golden Lions and flopped monumentally. Free State, unlucky losers of the 1997 Currie Cup final, did not make the semi-finals in 1998 and their union subsided into bankruptcy.

The Blue Bulls, as Northern Transvaal had become during 1998, steadily became better and better. Natal had their moments and Western Province made a comeback, but the most spectacular performance was by Griquas, winning the Vodacom Cup for provincial sides while the Springboks were playing the Tri-Nations, and becoming the first team to qualify for the Currie Cup semi-finals.

For Mallett, South Africa's poor Super 12 was a massive disappointment. He had to pick up his Springboks, who had walked tall when they got home from the 1997 Europe campaign and get them ready for the Tri-Nations. New Zealand teams had performed superbly at Super 12 time and the Wallabies had benefited under creative Rod Macqueen as coach. To make matters worse, the Springboks would start the Tri-Nations away – against the Wallabies in Perth and the All Blacks in windy Wellington.

Mallett had to find a replacement for Dick Muir, the veteran whose test career had come to an end, the steadying influence in the back line, the co-ordinator who got people into the right positions to attack and defend, the centre who brought out the best in Henry Honiball. In his place Mallett brought in Pieter Müller, almost a forgotten man in South African rugby.

Müller had been Danie Gerber's partner in 1992, but his international career appeared to have ended in 1993. He then opted for rugby league in Australia. With the disintegration of the amateur principle in 1995, Müller returned to rugby union, this time playing for Toulouse in the south-west of France from where Natal bought him home.

Mallett chose Müller, with his physical presence to dominate opposition, to do just that. It was an inspired choice as it turned out.

NORTHERN HEMISPHERE TOURISTS

Before the Tri-Nations the Springboks played four tests in South Africa – two against the feisty Irish, one against sad Wales and one against England who were coming back from their hidings in Australia and New Zealand, limping home with a team that had started off dilapidated as the top clubs refused to release their men for national duty.

The Springboks gathered on 6 June for the start of the 1998 campaign. It kicked off in inhospitable Bloemfontein where, yet again, the old flag flew and, yet again, the locals were rude to the Springboks. In 1960 they had spat on Lionel Wilson when he was chosen at fullback ahead of some local hero. Once more, they voiced crude dissatisfaction with the Springbok team which had only two Free Staters in it.

The Ireland tests were both unhappy – tawdry replicas of the bygone days of rugby violence. The Springboks won them easily enough but at the cost of dignity.

Before the Bloemfontein test Mallett warned that people should not expect too good a showing from the Springboks as during the preceding week he had worked them relentlessly at three training sessions. He was really looking to the Tri-Nations.

For the test Mallett chose two new boys – Stefan Terblanche and Gaffie du Toit – both young, both just starting their careers, both country boys on their way to becoming famous rugby players.

Gaffie du Toit suffered mightily. Within five minutes he had broken ribs and a gashed head as Paddy Johns, the Irish captain, led the charge on him. It was Du Toit's only test of the year, though the big flyhalf had some magnificent moments in Currie Cup rugby with his massive left boot and devastating break.

For Stefan Terblanche his début was a dream. He equalled the record of Chester Williams and Pieter Rossouw in scoring four tries but became the first Springbok to do so on début as he powered for the line at speed, strong on his feet.

The fighting of that test carried over to the second test against Ireland in Pretoria when the Springboks' discipline slipped in unacceptable ways, though they won 33-0 without danger of defeat. There was nothing in the test to be pleased with or proud of. Both tests were a disgrace.

Then there was Wales – poor, suffering Wales, still divided and robbed of its best players through bickering and selfishness. They toured and lost – to the likes of Border and to a Natal pick-up team.

Then came the test. The score, 96-13, was the biggest walloping in a match between nations of the old IRB (International Rugby Board) eight. The Welshmen left the scene disconsolate. Nick Mallett expressed his disappointment and disbelief that a side from proud Wales could be so poor.

The northern hemisphere performances were so bad that the southern nations decided they would have no more of it. Loftus Versfeld hosted two tests (the Welsh and the second Irish one) and lost some R3 million. Spectators did not want to watch second-best.

The England test was a mess at a sludgy Newlands where the drains refused to work on a field that had not recovered from a muddy match with the Irish four weeks before. England were simply not in the game, although they defended well. It was not a match to set blood racing, and the Springboks won 18-0.

A summary of the four matches played against northern hemisphere teams in South Africa is as follows:

P	W	D	L	Pf	Pa	Tf	Ta
4	4	0	0	184	26	28	2

The Springboks scored more tries than their opponents scored points!

TRI-NATIONS

Australia and New Zealand kicked off the Tri-Nations before a huge crowd at the Melbourne Cricket Ground and immediately there was an upset. The Wallabies won 24-16 and deserved better. The All Blacks looked bemused, especially in the centre. But nobody was ready for what was to come.

The Springboks' 1998 Tri-Nations started in Perth, the first-ever test in the Western Australian capital. The ground at Subiaco, in the heart of Australian Rules territory, was packed. The local media advertised the match as 'The Best on Earth in Perth', and many expatriate South Africans were there, happy to display their origins. The rain came down.

Before the match started, Gary Teichmann took the microphone and, in a touching moment, wished President Mandela a happy 80th birthday from the Springboks.

The Springboks, by a miracle of great, aggressive defence and conservative use of the boot when in possession – and some uncharacteristically wayward kicking by Australia's Matt Burke – won 13-12. Burke's last miss was from in front of the posts in the dying minutes of the match. The Wallabies scored two tries to one, the latter a slightly odd one where Joost van der Westhuizen took a ball from a ballboy at a penalty, tapped and scored while the Wallabies were left wondering. And yet the Springboks probably deserved victory – their first away Tri-Nations win after four defeats in the first two series.

The man of the match, so people said, was Pieter Müller, with his recklessly intimidatory presence in the centre. Opponents were not going to bash the ball past the Springbok inside trio of Joost van der Westhuizen, Henry Honiball and Müller. It was an important victory, and Mallett smiled. But he said that it was the worst Springbok performance during his term as coach. Result aside, it was not a test to remember.

Off the Springboks went to Wellington and John Hart's All Blacks, the Incomparables. They were without Frank Bunce, Zinzan Brooke and Sean Fitzpatrick, but New Zealand had such depth. Look at the way they had run the Super 12, ending with an all-New Zealand final.

Wellington, at the bottom of North Island, is the windy capital of New Zealand, a city of bays and rolling hills. It also has the most ramshackle test ground in the rugby world. In 1981 the Springboks had been victorious there, but had not won again in New Zealand, losing seven and drawing one of subsequent tests in the Land of the Long White Cloud. It was the 50th test between rugby's greatest rivals.

Surprisingly the weather was good – sunny with just a light breeze.

The Springboks defended for 60 minutes – bravely, aggressively, thoughtfully, patiently, passionately. And at the end of all their attacks the All Blacks had three meagre points to show for their efforts. The attacks grew more frantic as they kept breaking on the rocklike defence, and then the All Blacks began to recede.

All Black Carlos Spencer, a controversial choice at flyhalf ahead of Andrew Mehrtens, missed five kicks at goal, but then Montgomery missed four. Monty only booted one over in the first half.

At half-time Nick Mallett spoke earnestly to his team. He told them: 'Today's the day you decide whether you want to be world champions.'

In the second half Mehrtens was cheered on as a replacement for Spencer. Mehrtens goaled a penalty to level the scores. The All Blacks did not score again. It was their lowest score in a test match since 1986, their first home defeat since June 1994.

The Springboks dominated the last twenty minutes, moved 6-3 ahead and then were rewarded with a special try as the calm and elegant Henry Honiball moved right, did a waggle and then played back to Pieter Rossouw as he came in from the left wing and cut through under the posts for a famous Springbok victory. Of all moments in 1998, that try gave Nick Mallett his greatest sense of relief.

At the end of 1998 and despite all the records which the Springboks had set, Mallett still regarded this match at Athletic Park in Wellington as the finest performance by his Springboks. 'It was my best result, better even than our record win over France last year.'

Joost van der Westhuizen against Australia in 1998's Tri-Nations series.

Gary Teichmann said after the match: 'It's our best win since the World Cup.'

Both defences on the day were ruthless, none more so than Pieter Müller's.

With two away matches and two wins, the Tri-Nations looked not only possible but in the bag.

South African rugby has always been at its most vulnerable when it is expected to succeed, but put the players' backs to the wall and they can fight and succeed where they are expected to fail. Overconfidence is the besetting sin of South African rugby. In addition to overconfidence, the Springboks were aware that this second match against the All Blacks, strange though it may seem, was irrelevant to the outcome of the Tri-Nations. That would be decided against the Wallabies at Ellis Park.

The third test of the Tri-Series produced one of the greatest upsets the world of rugby football has ever known, a dozen minutes of miracle that left the doughty All Blacks in tears. It was a turn-around even bigger than that of the third test in 1965 when the suffering Springboks were down 16-5 at half-time and went on to win 19-16.

With 12 minutes to go, the All Blacks led 23-5. The Springboks were dead in the water. King's Park's enthusiastic crowd was quiet. Then came a fightback such as rugby has never seen. It ended with James Dalton scoring a try that won the match for the Springboks 24-23. It was the World Cup 'surge of the nation' feeling all over again. But Mallett was not satisfied and gave his men blazes for playing for only 20 minutes of 80, not revealing their full potential.

Lucky? The Springboks did score four tries to two, often a winning margin.

The next morning the Springboks and the All Blacks played golf at the Mt Edgecombe Country Club, Mallett's idea to try, in the age of professionalism, to get players socialising. The idea had actually come from John Hart when Mallett had met him in New Zealand, and Mallett organised it for the day after the Durban test.

To their credit 16 New Zealanders 'fronted up', as they would say, and played against 16 South Africans. Mallett and Teichmann played against Hart and Sean Fitzpatrick (the All Blacks' ex-captain) who played instead of Taine Randell (current captain of the All Blacks) who was not a golfer. Hart and Fitzpatrick won on the 18th. Both teams produced prizes, which were handed out. It was an amiable afternoon.

Mallett had got on well with both rival coaches, Hart of New Zealand and Rod Macqueen of Australia. When he watched the Super 12 match between the Coastal Sharks and the New South Wales Waratahs in Sydney, he sat with Macqueen and his fellow selectors. Mallett believes that the teams reflected the integrity of the coaches. There was not a single yellow card in the Tri-Nations Championship. It was vigorous but honest rugby.

Later when Hart was under pressure in New Zealand, Mallett wrote to sympathise, aware that the Springboks could quite easily have lost both tests to the All Blacks and that the Tri-Nations could easily have had a very different outcome. Hart wrote back thanking Mallett and expressing the hope that the tradition of post-test golf between the two countries could continue, perhaps in Dunedin in 1999.

And so to a packed Ellis Park and the last match of the Tri-Nations. The All Blacks had returned home and lost 27-23 to the Wallabies at Eden Park in Auckland, which meant that a Wallaby victory at Ellis Park would give the Australians victory. If Australia had won and South Africa had not scored a bonus point, Australia would have had 14 points to South Africa's 13.

But the Wallabies never looked like winning, and the Springboks were victorious with a final score of 29-15. The moment of utter brilliance came as Bobby Skinstad, in a centre position, sold a silly dummy to a man cutting back inside and then knifed through the Wallaby defence and round for a dive and a try at the posts. That clinched it.

The Springboks were the Best Team in the World! After 1995 they were the winners of the World Cup, the World Champions. Now they were the best in the world. Nick Mallett claimed that honour for his team. He also called them 'the luckiest team in the Tri-Nations'.

Gary Teichmann, the Man of the Series, proudly held the trophy aloft that proved that his Springboks deserved the title.

It was a sea change for the Springboks. In the previous two Tri-Nations series they had won a total of two matches. So had the Wallabies. The All Blacks had clinched all eight. This time the All Blacks won none, the Wallabies two and the Springboks all four. This impressive Tri-Nations victory was not received with anything like the national outpouring of joy that greeted the World Cup victory. And yet, in rugby terms, winning the Tri-Nations is a greater feat. To secure the 1995 World Cup, South Africa had to

A COMPARISON OF THE TRI-NATIONS LOGS OF 1996, 1997 AND 1998

1996

	P	W	D	L	Pf	Pa	Bonus Pts	Pts
New Zealand	4	4	0	0	119	60	1	17
South Africa	4	1	0	3	70	84	2	6
Australia	4	1	0	3	71	116	2	6

1997

	P	W	D	L	Pf	Pa	Bonus Pts	Pts
New Zealand	4	4	0	0	159	109	2	18
South Africa	4	1	0	3	148	144	3	7
Australia	4	1	0	3	96	150	2	6

1998

	P	W	D	L	Pf	Pa	Bonus Pts	Pts
South Africa	4	4	0	0	80	54	1	17
Australia	4	2	0	2	79	82	2	10
New Zealand	4	0	0	4	65	88	2	2

beat Australia and New Zealand once each. To win the Tri-Nations trophy, South Africa beat New Zealand and Australia twice each, at a time when they were without doubt two of the strongest three rugby countries in the world.

The downfall of New Zealand was remarkable – from top of the Tri-Nations log to the bottom in a year, which lent credence to the belief that it was not possible to stick with the same team past its sell-by date, that the hardest time to change is when you are doing well, that there is so much competition at the top that a bit of luck was all that stood between winning and losing, that real stars are scarce and not easily replaced.

Mallett said: 'Winning the Tri-Nations is the biggest rugby feat possible. The World Cup is a grand occasion, but the Tri-Nations is far harder. You play the equivalent of four World Cup finals in six weeks. The teams this year were so evenly matched that anyone could have won. I had hoped that we would win the Tri-Nations but never for a moment imagined that we would be unbeaten. The players deserve the praise. We may also have had a bit of luck, like Spencer and Burke missing a few kicks. And the All Blacks had lost a few leaders, but they have talent available and will be back.'

Noble Henry Honiball looks to pass at Lansdowne Road, Ireland, in 1998.

1998 TOUR

The 1998 tour to the United Kingdom and Ireland promised to be different. Mallett was more settled in command and the Springboks were coming off a great 1998. All sorts of records could be broken by the Springboks: as a team, they could surpass the record for consecutive victories of 17, held by the All Blacks (between the fourth test against the Springboks in 1965 and the first test against them in 1970); Mark Andrews could become the most capped Springbok; Gary Teichmann the most capped Springbok captain. Teichmann could also increase his number of consecutive caps and Joost van der Westhuizen his record number of test tries. They could also bring South Africa's record of Grand Slam victories to five.

The Grand Slam, a relatively new concept for touring teams, originated with the Wallabies in 1984 when they beat England, Ireland, Scotland and Wales. To a side touring from the southern hemisphere it meant achieving victory over the Four Home Unions (England, Scotland, Ireland and Wales) in a single tour. Amongst Five Nations teams of the northern hemisphere, it meant gaining victory over all four of the other participating nationss, an achievement accomplished by France, for the second year in a row, at the beginning of 1998.

The Springboks had achieved the Grand Slam on four successive tours – 1912-13, 1931-32, 1951-52 and 1960-61. On the demo tour of 1969, by contrast, they had failed to win a test, drawing with Wales and Ireland and losing the other two.

In 1998, the Springboks arrived in the United Kingdom and everybody expected them to win. In the previous year they had beaten England and Ireland twice each and comfortably, and they had had massive victories over Wales and Scotland. But somehow this year the aura of greatness eluded them.

They settled into the Westbury Hotel in London and practised at the Royal Artillery Ground, next to the Thames. It was all familiar ground to them and everything seemed in place.

But it did not quite work. From the Westbury Hotel, with its new, less friendly management, to the spirit in the team, things had changed.

A measure of provincialism had crept into the team. This may have been the result of the Springboks leaving five days after the most competitive Currie Cup season of all time, a period when provincialism is rife and lauded as a virtue in South African rugby. After five weeks of crunch games as the teams eliminated each other, it reached its climax in a thrilling final at Loftus Versfeld when the Blue Bulls beat Western Province.

The provincial composition of the Springbok team had changed. There were more Western Province players in the team, more English-speakers. Even though there was clear logic behind every single one of Mallett's selections, this led to suspicions and accusations, articulated mainly in *Die Beeld*, a Gauteng newspaper. Suggestions were levelled of English-speaking bias on Mallett's part and prejudice against certain players. Hennie Brandt, *Die Beeld's* rugby reporter, was reported as saying that he would blow Mallett and his 'English management' out of the water, a charge he afterwards denied, though four people reported that he said it. He later said that he had no reservations about Mallett or his management team, or about the fact that most of them spoke English as their first language. He also claimed that some of the misrepresentation came from Willie Pretorius of *Die Beeld's* London office, who took seriously a jesting remark made by Mallett about James Dalton.

Dalton had hurt his hamstring working out on a treadmill without warming up adequately. Mallett had said, in jest, of James: 'Sometimes his enthusiasm is not allied to his intelligence.'

Mallett himself spoke English to the players, who spoke whatever language they liked. He had no objection to Afrikaans. 'If you're selecting a word in such a way that you want to touch someone's heart, your home language is easier'. He believed that language was not an issue in the team.

> THE 1998 TOURING TEAM WAS: Percy Montgomery, Gaffie du Toit, Lourens Venter, Robert Markram, Pieter Rossouw, Stefan Terblanche, Breyton Paulse, Robbie Fleck, Christian Stewart, André Snyman, Deon Kayser, Franco Smith, Braam van Straaten, Henry Honiball, Joost van der Westhuizen, Werner Swanepoel, Chad Alcock, Gary Teichmann (captain), André Vos, Johan Erasmus, André Venter, Corné Krige, Bobby Skinstad, Philip Smit, Johnny Trytsman, Selborne Boome, Krynauw Otto, Mark Andrews, Adrian Garvey, Ollie le Roux, Toks van der Linde, Robbie Kempson, Willie Meyer, James Dalton, Naka Drotské, Owen Nkumane.

Brent Moyle joined the side when Willie Meyer returned home because of the tragic death of his baby daughter. Just as Corné Krige dropped out through injury in 1997, so Pieter Müller withdrew in 1998 to be replaced by Christian Stewart.

To break the players down into home languages is probably a silly exercise. In some cases the home language is obviously English, in other cases obviously Afrikaans and in one case probably neither. In some cases it is difficult to determine home language or usually used language. It is unlikely that anybody, bar a paranoid, would get worried if a third of the 1998 touring team have English as their home language! It's a smaller proportion than in 1937, when the Springbok team was also successful. When Mallett coached Boland, the team was overwhelmingly Afrikaans-speaking, which appeared to have created no problems at all.

The whole business seemed a malicious stirring-up of controversy around a team that was, disappointingly for some, free of controversy.

The language/provincial issue was not the only feeding place for *Die Beeld's* hunger for sensationalism. It also claimed that the team was snubbing SARFU officials, especially Mickey Gerber, the convener of selectors who had been sent over by SARFU for three weeks, and Keith Parkinson, the president of Natal Rugby Union and SARFU's junior vice-president. Gerber said afterwards that he had no complaint against Mallett but felt that the management team should have looked after his needs. Asked by Brandt what his complaints were, Parkinson said it was a personal matter. Natal, especially through Brian van Zyl, its chief executive officer, accused Alan Solomons of abusing his position by luring players, particularly Robbie Kempson, to Western Province, an allegation which Solomons strenuously denied, lodging the matter with his lawyers.

Mallett was convinced that officials were welcome to travel but should stay in separate hotels and leave the team alone. Nick Mallett's job was to coach and manage the South African rugby side, not look after SARFU's officials, however fond he might be of them. He felt that it was simply beyond management's responsibility and capability to care for them and their arrangements.

Brandt also said that he had inside information that suggested that ill-feeling between Mallett and Dalton existed, that Mallett was angry with Dalton's performance in the Irish test and remarked that 'it is buzzing here [Belfast] after it became known that an injured Springbok rugby player, the hooker James Dalton, can possibly return to South Africa this week'. He went on: 'Although it is officially being said that it is an injury which can mean the end of his tour in Britain, there is speculation that there is perhaps another reason.' Mallett believed that he had the best medical team in world rugby. Deciding on Dalton's fitness was a matter for them. They, not Mallett, had decided that Dalton should leave the field.

Mallett saw Brandt going down a passage and called him for a chat. Brandt professed to having no problem with Mallett's management or his treatment of players and did not believe that he was at all biased or prejudiced. It was odd that the only suggestion of press aggression against Mallett and the Springboks should come from a South African journalist at a time when the British press, notoriously hostile to visiting teams, were giving the Springboks magnificent coverage.

For their first match, South Africa's second team, or Dirt Trackers, went up to Glasgow, stayed in Troon and played the Glasgow Caledonians at Firhill Stadium in Glasgow, since 1909 the ground of Partick Thistle, a second division soccer club. The stadium'scapacity is 19 000 but fewer than 2 500 people sat on the Main Stand to watch the match between the Springboks and Glasgow Caledonians, a regional Scottish team participating in Europe's rugby competition without great success. They had, with their full side, been comprehensively beaten by Pontypridd, a Welsh club, and they did not have their full team against the Springboks.

The test team remained in London and watched it on television at the BBC studios.

The Springboks were never in danger of losing but spluttered mightily. Every now and again they scored a try but never exerted full dominance. Their forwards were a loose lot. Best of the Caledonians was John Leslie, the Kiwi who had only just arrived in Scotland and who was destined to play against the Springboks in the test. Leslie was not the only foreigner in the side. Luke Smith, a South African, was at flyhalf and Tommy Hayes, who played in New Zealand but had represented the Cook Islands in a World Cup qualifier, was at fullback. For South Africa, Breyton Paulse impressed with his speed and Bobby Skinstad became the youngest player ever to captain the Springboks. Braam van Straaten had a strong match, especially with his boot, till he left the field after being viciously raked in the face by Jason White, the Caledonian flank, who was later cited and suspended for 116 days. The hearing was held in Glasgow, by which time all the Springboks were back in London for the Wembley test.

Scott Quinnell received friendlier treatment. Brian Campbell, the test referee, had sent him off the field for a late tackle on Lawrence Dallaglio while playing for Richmond against Wasps in a club match. His suspension would have ruled him out of the Welsh test against South Africa, but he appealed and was allowed to play while his appeal was heard. He missed the date of the first hearing because his wife was giving birth in Llanelli, and thus he ended up playing in the test. He would receive a yellow card in the test but his monstrous high tackle on Gary Teichmann was overlooked. Some of the Welsh tackling was really assault.

WEMBLEY THRILLER

The Springbok-Welsh test was played at Wembley, as the Welsh were rushing to finish the brand-new Millennium Stadium in Cardiff in time for the 1999 Rugby World Cup.

The weather was good, the field in perfect condition in the great stadium with the London Welsh Male Voice Choir singing to get the spirit going – quite different from the *Hier Kom die Bokke* razzmatazz of Ellis Park but it worked up *hwyl*, the Welshman's special spirit. Most of the singing was hymnal but there was also *Delilah*, a Cardiff Arms Park favourite, transported to Wembley for the occasion.

The test was a close-run affair, a thriller. Several aspects to the test suggested that the Springboks, for all their organisation and planning, for all their previous victories, were fragile indeed. Wales sailed into them with a spirit they had not shown for years and with creativity, the hallmark of the coaching of Graham Henry. It had not taken them long to learn to play the Auckland way.

Wales scored a magnificent try as they poured through the Springbok midfield where Pieter Müller was more missed than people would have imagined. Neil Jenkins kicked three penalty goals while the Springboks eschewed kicks at goal in search of tries – without success. Then they had a scrum to the right of the Welsh goal posts and a few metres from the line. They shoved forward. Jonathan Humphreys popped up in the middle of the front row, the scrum wheeled a bit and the referee went off to award a penalty try. From the kick-off the Springboks launched a full attack, at speed and this time with sure hands, and Joost van der Westhuizen went over for a try. That brought the score to 14-all at half-time.

In the second half the Welsh came into Springbok territory from time to time, the Springboks conceded penalties and Wales went ahead. The Boks caught up to 20-all after 80 minutes of the match had passed. Then in injury time Scott Quinnell, whose behaviour on the field was often wayward, conceded a penalty for which he received a yellow card and again the Springboks went for the try. They won the line-out and instead of peeling wide played back to Joost van der Westhuizen on the touch-line side. He sneaked through a gap, came close to scoring, popped the ball inside where it eluded Rassie Erasmus but was snatched up by André Venter for a try.

It was not the end of the game as, apart from injuries, there had also been a long stoppage to remove an athletic streaker with a good side-step. It turned out that he was a South African, Oliver Gibbs from Port Elizabeth, and there were suggestions that Mallett rope him into the side as soon as possible. He had the longest and most elusive run of any South African on the day!

Final score: 28-20 to South Africa.It was a thrilling match that deserved more than the 53 000 who came to watch, leaving some 26 000 empty seats. Wales came out of it with vast honour, and the United Kingdom and Ireland rejoiced.

The Springboks had fumbled and missed tackles. They had restrained themselves in many brutal attacks, which were largely outside of the laws as they were still aware of Mallett's condemnation of their violence in the second test against Ireland earlier in the year. The Springboks who came in for especial criticism were Adrian Garvey, Mark Andrews and Rassie Erasmus in the pack and Franco Smith, Stefan Terblanche and Percy Montgomery behind the scrum.

In speaking of the match afterwards, Mallett said: 'I underestimated the ability of the Welsh to play the sort of game Graham Henry coaches.' Henry had an excellent and detailed knowledge of South African rugby. His team avoided line-outs, ran with ball in hand, especially wide, drove round the fringes and jumped on Joost van der Westhuizen whenever they could.

Mallett said his side had been 'shocking'. 'The players should be professional enough to know that when something is not working, you change it on the field. It took us 60 minutes to change something we should have after ten.'

Mallett then made it clear to the mid-week side that the door of opportunity had been kicked open for them. He believed that his team had functioned badly because he had opted for the wrong plan and that the test players deserved a second chance for that reason, but he told them their places were in jeopardy.

In this test, Mark Andrews became the first Springbok ever to play 50 tests and he had the honour of leading the side out in a special jersey. Gary Teichmann became South Africa's most capped captain in his record 35th consecutive test, and Nick Mallett, with his 14th successive victory as coach, equalled the record held by Fred Allen and Kitch Christie. On the other hand, Wales maintained their record of never beating the Springboks and never scoring more than a solitary try against them.

SCOTLAND

Next the Dirt Trackers moved to Edinburgh to take on the Edinburgh Reivers, the other professional, regional side in Scotland, with players from several different clubs. As was the case with the Glasgow Caledonians, the Reivers did not have their full side, as five were in the Scottish squad.

Reiver is a Scottish word meaning 'robber, plunderer, pirate'. But they did not steal much from the Springboks at Easter Road Stadium (capacity 16 000) – the Hibernian soccer ground for more than a century – which was almost devoid of spectators, as only 1 463 people braved the freezing weather to watch the Springboks win comfortably. The conditions were perfect – good underfoot and windless. But in a sense it was another meaningless match – against an under-strength northern hemisphere team. The Caledonians and the Reivers both played against the Maoris and the Springboks. The total try count against them was 34 and they scored no tries themselves. There was now the oddity of the Springboks playing under-strength touring teams from northern hemisphere countries and then again under-strength northern hemisphere teams when they themselves were on tour.

But it did give Mallett the opportunity to experiment. He started with Christian Stewart at flyhalf and Braam van Straaten at inside centre. Van Straaten played the first half and looked uncomfortable. In the second half Mallett whipped Stewart off and put him into the Springbok squad in place of Franco Smith. His other change was to remove André Venter to the bench – a massive surprise. In came Bob Skinstad as flank, who had been expected rather to replace Rassie Erasmus who had had a mediocre test against Wales. Mallett said that Venter, for all his dependability and

Scottish Springboks? Krynauw Otto, Stefan Terblanche and Mark Andrews in Edinburgh in 1998.

effort, had an 'old-fashioned look' about him. Mallett would have preferred him at lock, but not to start with. It was a dramatic move. Previously Mallett had stuck by his family-squad, and changes had been forced through injury, except for James Small, the only player Mallett had previously dropped. He spent a sleepless night worrying about dropping Venter after the Reivers' match, but believed he was doing the right thing, regardless of the opposition for the next match. He needed greater solidity in the centre than Franco Smith had offered and the greater attacking ability of Skinstad. What worried him was upsetting the spirit within his family-squad.

Strange how things happen. There was enormous upset when François Pienaar was not chosen at the end of 1996, though the sportswriters of South Africa had not included him amongst their top ten players of a year in which they included four other loose-forwards in the group. Venter was universally acknowledged as a top flank. The leading New Zealand magazine, *Rugby Monthly*, rated him the top flank in the world, above even their own Josh Kronfeld. Yet Venter's omission was greeted with bewilderment, not the anger that greeted Pienaar's omission.

There may be several reasons for this – the country's trust in Mallett, Pienaar's special position in the nation's psyche or the fact that the Springboks were winning in 1998 while they had been losing in 1996. Certainly people are more tolerant of a winning team than of a losing one. Mallett, of course, articulated his reasons. He spent a long time with Venter before he announced the team, explaining his thinking and explaining how he saw him as the athletic lock which modern rugby required.

To Mallett, it was ridiculous not to pick Bobby Skinstad. The whole world, so it seemed, was bemused that he was not selected, the form flank, a miracle worker. Some even felt he should have been in ahead of Johan Erasmus but the two were never in competition for the Number 6 jersey: Erasmus' job was at close quarters; Skinstad was simply not that sort of player.

Mallett had been experimenting with Venter at lock during the season and when he came on in that position against Scotland, he had a massive impact on the game. Venter was disappointed at first but Mallett said of him: 'André Venter is a fantastic person. It took him time to come to terms with the change but when I explained it to him and explained his part in the team, he understood. He will give it his best punt and is certainly in my plans for 1999.'

As Mallett saw it, South Africa had at least eight first-class flanks, but only two locks. Krynauw Otto and Mark Andrews had played together in 17 tests but they were the only two top locks in the country with young Selborne Boome on the way up. He could not immediately replace Andrews or Otto with Venter in the hope that he was going to be as good as they were, but he could introduce him gradually in the expectation of taking four top locks to the World Cup in 1999.

The result against Scotland was, in all conscience, solid enough, but Scotland had had a poor record with only a scraped home win over Ireland to show for any 1998 success and a 51-26 defeat by Fiji, and were beset with internal problems. Certain rugby men in Scotland were rebelling against what they saw as the tyrannical regime of Duncan Paterson, the ex-international who became chairman of the Scottish Rugby

Union's executive board, the only elected board in world rugby to pay itself. Crowds at matches were poor. The Springboks, despite a better 1998 than 1997, attracted only half the turn-out to Murrayfield – 29 765 in a ground with a capacity of 67 500.

Before the match the teams were introduced to the Princess Royal, whose son Peter Philips had been a flank with the Scottish Schools team which toured South Africa and who was captaining the Scotland Under 21 team in 1998.

Again the Springboks struggled as the Scots kept possession and the Springboks lost it. The Scots led 7-3 after Hodge had scored a try. The Springboks plodded on lethargically, content to tackle and wait for mistakes. But they did construct two tries of their own in rare flashes of glory and scored another three by forcing the Scots into errors. Skinstad scored a try of great majesty as he strode 50 metres down the middle of Murrayfield and Van der Westhuizen showed all his skill and opportunism in poaching the ball at a tackle and sniping half the length of the field for a try. Terblanche, who had a quiet tour after the explosive start to his international career, scored a magnificently constructed try. The Springboks won 35-10, but it was not a convincing performance.

Victory over Scotland meant that Nick Mallett was a record-breaking coach – passing the 14 consecutive victories of Fred Allen and Kitch Christie. Of the 14 All Blacks' victories under Allen, eight were at home. Of the Springboks' victories under Christie, 10 were at home. Of the Springboks 16 victories under Mallett, six were at home. In the case of Allen and Christie they always played against full-strength teams. The

STATS OF RECORD-BREAKING COACHES ALLEN, CHRISTIE & MALLETT

Fred Allen	Kitch Christie	Nick Mallett
Lions, 20-3	Argentina, 42-22	Italy, 62-31
Lions, 16-12	Argentina, 46-26	France, 36-32
Lions, 19-6	Scotland, 34-10	France, 52-10
Lions, 24-11	Wales, 20-12	England, 29-11
Australia, 29-9	Western Samoa, 60-8	Scotland, 68-10
England, 23-11	Australia, 27-18	Ireland, 37-13
Wales, 13-6	Romania, 21-8	Ireland, 33-0
France, 21-15	Canada, 20-0	Wales, 96-13
Scotland, 14-3	Western Samoa, 42-14	England, 18-0
Australia, 27-11	France, 19-15	Australia, 14-13
Australia, 19-18	New Zealand, 15-12	New Zealand, 13-3
France, 12-9	Wales, 40-11	New Zealand, 24-23
France, 9-3	Italy, 40-21	Australia, 29-15
France 19-12	England, 24-14	Wales, 28-20
		Scotland, 35-10
		Ireland, 27-13

Mallett makes a point. Backing him up are Montgomery, Kempson and Swanepoel.

Welsh and English sides, which toured South Africa in 1998, were not full-strength teams. But Australia and New Zealand certainly were.

Unfortunately there was an unpleasant aftermath to the Scottish test. After the victory the Springboks went on the town to the Dome, a night-club. Initially several were refused entry, for being dressed too casually or because the management feared the depredations of a rugby team, but eventually virtually the whole squad was in the Dome. Then things went awry. Two of the back-up team, David Dobela and Julius Mathatho, were abused by somebody passing as a Scottish supporter who called them *kaffirs*, told them rudely to go off home and pushed them about. Henry Honiball came to the rescue and warned the unpleasant Scot that there were several Springboks who wished to chat to him. He retreated and the Springboks left.

The media reported the incident. Mallett spoke out against it. 'I don't want any special treatment. What I want is common decency and that each of my squad is respected as an individual. The racist remarks anger me the most. Racism is never acceptable. I would not tolerate it from one of my players. Why must we tolerate it because the abuser is Scottish?'

The Scots reacted quickly and Charlie Laidlaw, a spokesman for the Scottish Rugby Union, apologised and assured the Springboks that they would be welcome in Edinburgh for the 1999 World Cup. Mallett was reported as intending to

143

write officially to the World Cup Organising Committee to ask that the Springboks be hosted elsewhere. The issue was blown out of proportion, enlarged because of the sensitivity to racism when South Africans are involved.

OVER TO IRELAND

The Springboks again hit trouble this selfsame weekend. They were happy to get the Aer Lingus charter to Cork in Ireland's deep south, where the welcome was warm. The Metropolis Hotel staff were friendly and a banner across MacCurtain Street welcomed the Springboks. And when the Springboks left the hotel, they sang to the staff and the staff sang to them before going outside to wave their guests goodbye, impressed by their good manners.

Late on the Sunday night after the team's arrival, a young woman went to the MacCurtain Street police station and reported a Springbok for assaulting her in a night-club. Her verbal report had said that when she had slapped one of the Springboks, he had grabbed her and told her that she should not hit him. Whereupon she had hit him again. He had immediately left and the woman, who did not appear at all sober, left the club and went to MacCurtain Street police station to report the matter. The policeman said it was a trivial matter and that they were not investigating.

The Springbok management looked into the matter and found it ridiculously trivial. But the press were onto it. Hennie Brandt reported it on the front page of *Die Beeld*. Some people found the Springboks' squeaky-clean image intolerable.

The match at Musgrave Road was the best for the mid-week Springboks. The ground was packed with 8 000 enthusiastic spectators. The Combined Provinces kept coming at the Springboks, and the Springbok Dirt Trackers responded with their best performance of the tour to win 32-5. Eddie Helvey's try for the Provinces was a marvel of intricacy at close quarters from a line-out.

Both matches in Ireland were played with an enthusiasm that was absent in Scotland.

Then it was Dublin and the Irish test with much hype about a reputation of on-field violence. Vengeance was possible. Ireland has seven centuries' practice at remembering past hurts. They say an Irishman has a bad memory – he doesn't forget.

The match was niggling but it did not get out of hand. Keith Wood and Peter Clohessy, a player with an unhappy record of misconduct, received yellow cards. So did Adrian Garvey for being punched by Clohessy.

The Springboks struggled inordinately. It was hard for them to get into the game as the penalties streamed against them. In all they were penalised 25 times to the dozen of Ireland. In his comment on the game Uli Schmidt said: 'It was hard to know who wanted Ireland to win most – the players, the spectators or the referee!'

As a result, the Springbok tries were long-range ones and all the more thrilling for being so. Just before half-time Rassie Erasmus, who had a magnificent match, did a shimmy, scurried through a gap in the centre and raced over 30 metres to score. Then in the second half the Springboks made the game safe. Within two minutes Bobby Skinstad had gone racing off on two long runs. The first time he went sweeping past Conor O'Shea, the Irish fullback, to score himself. On the second occasion, he scooped up the ball as Joost van der Westhuizen robbed the Irish of the ball at a scrum which they had won. Skinstad then passed to Honiball who threw a long pass to Van der Westhuizen for a straight run for the posts. They were two moments of great individualism by the glamorous flank.

The Irish believed their tight forwards were the best in the world, but the Springboks did everything better than they did, save only in the line-outs.

The Springbok victory meant they had now drawn level with the All Blacks, who had established the record of 17 consecutive test victories between 1965 and 1970. New Zealand had done so under four different captains – Wilson Whineray, Brian Lochore, Chris Laidlaw and Kel Tremain. Gary Teichmann had been the Springboks' captain throughout, and he celebrated the occasion with a better performance than he had managed against Wales and Scotland.

Only three captains have captained their teams in victories over all the senior IRB countries – Will Carling, Nick Farr-Jones and Gary Teichmann. The latter two achieved the feat away from home. Teichmann has, by some way, the record for the most consecutive test victories for a national captain.

The Dirt Trackers had one more match left – against Ireland A, who were expected to be their best opposition on the tour.

This match, played in a Belfast mist before a capacity crowd of 9 000 – for the third successive time in Ireland – was won by the South Africans more easily than even the score of 50-19 suggests. But the Springboks suffered mightily at the hands of the referee. The penalty count ran 28-8 against them. Nonetheless, the Springboks dominated from start to finish and the only time the Irish threatened them was six minutes from the end when a penalty got them a line-out near the Springbok goal-line and a try resulted.

The most pleasing aspect of the match, from a South African point of view, was the display of Gaffie du Toit who was secure and inventive in the unpleasant weather, justifying Mallett's belief that he had the makings of a great fullback.

The Dirt Trackers, as they call themselves with pride, completed their first unbeaten tour since South Africa's re-entry into world rugby in 1992. Their record on this tour was impressive:

P	W	D	L	Pf	Pa	Tf	Ta
4	4	0	0	193	36	30	2

Points were made up as follows:

	T	C	D	P
Dirt Trackers:	30	20	0	1
Opposition:	2	1	0	8

And so to the last round-up of the tour, to the fateful meeting at Twickenham, the season's last hurrah and also the chance for the Springboks to set a record that was likely to stand forever.

THE FIRST DEFEAT

South Africa, as always, expected so much of its Springboks, and the Springboks, as always, were most vulnerable when they were hot favourites, in this case expected to break the All Blacks record of 17 successive victories as a prelude to moving that record into the realms of the unattainable.

It was not to be.

Springbok hands let them down. The match was played at close quarters and England excelled there. Chances were lost or eschewed, England defended and the Springboks had one of their longest passages ever without scoring a point. And in the end England became 'World Beaters'.

That there was such English euphoria was a massive compliment to the Springboks. To beat the Springboks meant to beat the best. But it was a hard defeat to swallow. Nobody in the rugby world enjoys losing to England. It is the one side everybody wants to beat, as they find rugby in England self-satisfied – the self-appointed custodians of taste and virtue, the harshest critics of visitors and the loudest trumpeters in victory.

The Springboks, used to victory, will have found defeat doubly hard. On 5 December 1998 the Springboks lost a test under Mallett for the first time – a scrappy test of many errors, but they lost well – especially Nick Mallett. He was graciousness itself.

The Twickenham test was a big occasion for England who had lost by a single point to the Wallabies the week before, after the Wallabies had comprehensively beaten France the week before that.

As was the case with the All Blacks in 1997, the Twickenham test was one too many. In 1997 England had drawn with the All Blacks. This time they beat the Springboks.

For Mallett it was not surprising. From the start of the tour he found it hard to lift his players. They might well have lost to Wales, and struggled against the lowly Scots. Their most convincing victory was over Ireland, but England was the one they really wanted to win. It just did not happen. As usual, they eschewed kicks at goal in the hope of scoring tries, without any success. They then opted for an easy kick at goal and Percy Montgomery missed it. England hoisted the Springboks with their own petard, kicking into touch instead of for goal and keeping the Springboks on the rack for a long, uncomfortable time. At the death, South Africa burst out of close defence and only a deflecting English hand, knocking down a pass, saved England. But throughout, the Springbok fliers had had hardly a sniff of the ball.

The players had told Mallett that they were ready for the England match and they assured him that they would lift their game, but they did not.

Mallett himself saw the record at the end of the road, predicting that, if they broke the All Black record, the one that the Springboks set would last forever. Records were in the forefront of their minds, and with records, a place in history.

However much the players, especially Teichmann, tried to put the records out of their minds, the fact remained that they were in the forefront of the players' minds. Mallett remarked afterwards that the effect was to make the players, especially the senior ones, more conservative. Eventually the outcome was decided by penalties and by opportunities taken and opportunities lost as much as by sticking to the team that had brought the Springboks to the brink of the new record.

Possibly the greatest harm done on the tour was to the reputation of the Springbok tight five. The four teams they played against ceased to fear the Springbok tight forwards.

Test summary:

P	W	D	L	Pf	Pa	Tf	Ta
4	3	0	1	97	56	12	4

The whole tour:

P	W	D	L	Pf	Pa	Tf	Ta
8	7	0	1	290	92	42	6

And then there were people who thought the tour was a flop!

A summary of tests under Mallett looks as follows:

17	16	0	1	608	230	82	9

Mallett had no doubt that northern hemisphere rugby had caught up. He felt he had been a year ahead at False Bay and then a year ahead at Boland and then a year ahead with the Springboks, but people steal with their eyes and catch up.

There was also the New Zealand influence on northern hemisphere rugby. Jim Telfer of Scotland was a New Zealand disciple. England's assistant coach, John Mitchell, was a New Zealander and the coaches of Wales and Ireland, Graham Henry and Warren Garland, were New Zealanders. There had been seven Welsh coaches in ten years before Graham Henry – Henry the Eighth! The evidence of the Springbok test and his players' reaction to him suggest that he had made an enormous difference. His arrival was heralded with a possibly blasphemous line from *Cym Rhondda* – Guide me, O thou great redeemer!

Northern hemisphere teams kept possession for longer periods, their defences were better organised and they picked the same sort of players that Mallett had chosen.

It would be fair to say that the 1999 Rugby World Cup in Europe will not be easy for southern hemisphere countries.

INJURIES & MONEY

A the end of the tour Nick Mallett's medical team reported that all of his test players were carrying injuries of some sort – some more serious than others. The serious ones were Joost van der Westhuizen's knee, Adrian Garvey's Achilles tendon, Christian Stewart's shoulder and neck, James Dalton's calves and Stefan Terblanche's elbow. Garvey, Van der Westhuizen and Stewart underwent surgery immediately on return, Garvey on the Monday following the England test. Joost van der Westhuizen spent Christmas Day in the Little Company of Mary Hospital in Pretoria after being operated on by Daan du Plessis, the former Springbok prop. He was hoping to play in the 1999 World Cup. Stewart had two operations – to his neck and his shoulder.

The injury report, drawn up by Dr Wayne Diesel at the end of the 1998 tour, looked alarming. His report said: 'The fact that every single member of the Test team against England had at least one injury, except for Bobby (and he had severe abdominal cramps on Friday evening) clearly proves that these players have all played too much rugby this season.' The only players in the whole squad of 37 who were entirely free from injury were Owen Nkumane, Breyton Paulse and Brent Moyle. Altogether 66 different injuries were treated, most of them in the lower back and thigh. Thirty-four of the injuries had occurred before the tour, 32 on tour.

It is obvious that the need to play fit people only is important, and it begs questions about the number of matches played, especially for the battered tight five who were certainly unable to lift their game for the Twickenham test.

Mallett believes that it is not the number of matches as much as the length of the season that counts, with the resultant brevity of recovery time. The Springboks were in hectic action from February to December 1998. In 1999 this would be repeated. He would like to see the Super 12 starting later and possibly in a different format, the Currie Cup ending in September and the end-of-year tour starting in October, not November. That would give the players November, December and part of January off.

At present rugby players have winter almost the whole year as they play in both hemispheres and time off can be less than a month. A 'global season' has been suggested. That would require the northern hemisphere to make rugby a summer game, with a season that lasted from the beginning of April till the end of September, allowing the players a proper rest.

It's hard to say how much money plays a part in the player's decision and determination to play, even with an injury.

The World Cup players had received huge contracts but many had petered out of the game afterwards. A new system was brought in, which included a basic wage and then added appearance money.

THE SPRINGBOKS WERE DIVIDED INTO THREE CATEGORIES AND PAID AS FOLLOWS:

A Category:	R700 000,00 per annum
B Category:	R600 000,00 per annum
C Category:	R500 000,00 per annum

Average rate of conversion as at January 1999:

US dollar	R6.0110
British pound	R9.9260
Australian dollar	R3.7946
New Zealand dollar	R3.2378

In all, 26 players fall into the different categories. The categories are reviewed every six months when players can change categories, be added to them or removed from them. The categories were again reviewed at the beginning of 1999 and recommendations made to SARFU.

In addition, for a test a Springbok would be paid R25 000,00 for being in the squad of 22. They would also get R3 000 each for a win, R5 000 if that win was against Australia or New Zealand.

The mid-week team had its own form of contract. They were paid R10 000,00 per week and R10 000, 00 per match played. They all played, or at least got onto the field, in all matches and so came home with R90 000 for their five weeks' work.

A lot of money? The taxman also gets a lot of it.

It has been thought that players were playing with injuries for fear of losing their match fees. The truth is that all players in all sports get injured. Players have always striven to play through injuries even in days when there was no payment involved. The question of injuries is always more likely to be posed when the team loses. The fact that the same players played with the same injuries in victory goes unnoticed.

Mallett would like SARFU to contract the top 120 players, who would then belong to SARFU and not to the unions. Come Super 12 time, SARFU would allot the players. There would not then be the anomaly of having James Dalton and Naka Drotské playing in the same Super 12 team and taking turns to play, which left both short of matches at the end of the year.

Mallett is happy that players be well paid. SARFU's money is generated primarily by the Super 12 and the Springboks. It is only fair that the money should go to those players.

Nick Mallett, with typical gesture, in earnest conversation with the press. One of Mallett's strongest points is that he is always available to talk to the media.

REFS AND PRESS

On a rugby tour and indeed in rugby generally, media men and referees are often seen as the enemy. From the start the media took to Nick Mallett. For one thing he was patently honest and dealt openly with them. Secondly, he always made himself available to journalists and always gave his comment. He was a media person's dream. For this reason, he was angered with Hennie Brandt of *Die Beeld*, who wrote that Mallett was cross with Dalton and his performance in the Irish test, which led to unhappiness between the two of them. Thirdly, he was not a 'no comment' man. He had his say, he said it clearly and he was worth quoting.

The British press gave the Springboks great coverage as a result, not just papers like *The Telegraph* and *The Times*, but also the *Daily Mirror* and the *Daily Express*. Eddie Butler of the BBC did an interview with Mallett to be shown on BBC Sport as part of the preview of the Welsh test. The BBC also ran a documentary on Mallett during the tour.

Much of the way the Springboks were received in the United Kingdom and Ireland was Mallett-created, especially the tone of the team, which they in part had developed following their meetings with Tim Southey. The Springboks were seen as gracious, friendly and humble. They did South Africa proud.

In his book *Great Games*, David Williams, an excellent commentator on matters sporting, summed up the Mallett era wonderfully: 'I began to be at peace again with rugby towards the end of 1997, when Nick Mallett became the first national coach to demonstrate a profound understanding of the deep importance of rugby, both as a game and in the political context of a bruised country that needs much healing. To our traditional grim determination was added a capacity for enjoyment, to perform at the highest level but also to relish the wind in your face and the rain on your eyelids.'

Mallett achieved all this with what seems like a form of political naïvety, which takes absolutely no notice of race. He would simply treat everybody in the same way. All he wanted to have, in his capacity as Springbok coach, was the freedom to pick the best team to represent South Africa in the best possible circumstances. Not that he was unaware of the need for social transformation in South Africa, which he welcomed. But he knew that only the best would be good enough to compete at international level with the likes of the All Blacks and the Wallabies. The form of transformation which he wanted was the sort that transforms the abilities of people through opportunity, education and training. To this process he was happy to commit himself.

He stated that a way to get players to the top was to identify them as schoolboys and then get them to attend the top rugby schools in the country on bursaries. 'I will find 30 businessmen who will pay for their education,' he said.

Political pressures, not just from government, are for Mallett an added problem which other coaches in the rugby world do not suffer. There is pressure on him to choose players on grounds other than just ability, but South Africa, with its legacy of apartheid, is simply not as homogenous as the rugby worlds of New Zealand, Australia, France, England, Argentina, Fiji and so on. Fortunately, his rapport with the new president of SARFU, Silas Nkanunu, is excellent.

AWARD

Pat Marshall, a rugby writer for the *Daily Express*, died prematurely in 1975, not long after covering the 1974 Lions' tour of South Africa. The Rugby Union Writers' Club instituted an award in his name, for the outstanding rugby personality of the year. The first award, in 1976, was to Mervyn Davies, the great Welsh Number 8, who had captained Wales to a Grand Slam and then suffered a brain haemorrhage which ended his career. He played 38 times for Wales and 78 times for the Lions. The award has been made each year since. All the members, the vast majority of whom are British, vote in October for the award, which is made at the annual dinner each January.

Before 1998 only one South African had received the award – François Pienaar in 1993-94.

In 1998, at the 38th annual dinner of the 400-strong Rugby Writers' Club, held at the Café Royal in London, Nick Mallett received the Pat Marshall Award for the Outstanding Rugby Personality of 1998. The award was handed over to him by the previous winner, Lawrence Dallaglio.

In receiving the award, Mallett said: 'It is always special to be honoured in this way. At the same time it is important to recognise the many other people who contributed to the success of the Springbok team over the past year. I would like to thank SARFU, my management team, the players and the spectators for their support. I hope that the award is not just for our results on the field but also for the way we have conducted ourselves off the field.' The last statement produced enthusiastic applause.

The list of award winners is impressive indeed, a litany of rugby greatness:

Mervyn Davies (1975–76), Andy Irvine (1976–7), Gareth Edwards (1977–78), JPR Williams (1978–79), Billy Beaumont (1979–80), Ollie Campbell (1981–82), Dave Loveridge (1982–83), Jim Aitken (1983–84), Mick Doyle, the Irish coach (1984–85), Jonathan Davies (1985–86), David Kirk (1986–87), Bob Norster (1987–88), Finlay Corder 1988–89), Ian McGeechan, the Scottish coach (1989–90), David Campese (1990–91), Nick Farr-Jones (1991–92), Ben Clarke (1992–93), François Pienaar (1993–94), Jonah Lomu (1994–95), Sean Fitzpatrick (1995–96), Lawrence Dallaglio (1996–97), Nick Mallett, the Springbok coach (1997–98).

Nick Mallett is the third national coach to receive the award after Mick Doyle and Ian McGeechan.

REFEREEING

Mallett has even managed to get on with referees, which may surprise many of his playing contemporaries!

'What now, sir?' Mallett the player would look up at the referee when the whistle went. There may have been a 'sir' on the end but the manner would remain aggressive. And yet for all that, as a player Mallett had a reasonable rapport with referees. As the Springbok coach, his behaviour towards referees has been impeccable, though it has not always been easy to keep a guard on his mouth.

Refereeing remains a problem for coaches. The coach watches a match almost solely from the position of his players and a match is frequently a time of emotional explosion. That explosion may, from time to time, be directed at the referee.

This has become less of a problem as many areas of law have been simplified – for example, the line-out, where the licence to lift a player has made the laws easier and the game more spectacular. The problem remains of what happens after the tackle, the area where most penalties are incurred and where most inconsistencies happen, and here the International Rugby Board could do well to pull in representatives of coaches and players when they review post-tackle laws.

It has been fashionable to make a distinction between northern hemisphere and southern hemisphere referees, with the northerners regarded as greater purists and therefore more pernickety when it come to the post-tackle situation.

Before the Welsh test Jonathan Davies, one of Wales's heroes of yesteryear, expressed regret that the referee, Stuart Dickinson of Australia, was from the southern hemisphere. He said: 'We need all the help we can get in the northern hemisphere.'

That is an astonishing statement. He felt that Wales were at an unfair disadvantage because the referee was from a different hemisphere. It is less a comment on the integrity of referees than on the state of refereeing throughout the world, or at least the perception of referees and refereeing.

Home venue is far more important than a referee's hemisphere of origin.

A comparison of home and away matches makes that point, for the Springboks were throughout the year the same team playing to the same laws, against the same opposition. On their 1998 tour, the Springboks were, in every single match, penalised more frequently than their opponents. When South Africa played at home, the ratio of penalties for to against was 55% to 45%. When South Africa played away from home, the ratio of penalties for to against was 40% to 60%. Statistics will show that the home team is penalised considerably less frequently than the visiting team.

The penalty count in matches involving the Dirt Trackers is even more lopsided.

On the 1998 tour Mallett had the impression that, although he insisted on the same discipline and manners from his players, there was a feeling that the Springboks had been at the top of the pile for too long and the tide of penalties raced in favour of the

A RECORD OF PENALTIES FOR AND AGAINST THE SPRINGBOKS IN 1998. THE SCORES GIVEN BELOW ARE PENALTIES IN FAVOUR. THE HOME TEAM IS MENTIONED FIRST.

South Africa	16	Ireland	11
South Africa	14	Ireland	17
Ireland	24	South Africa	14
South Africa	14	Wales	11
Wales	16	South Africa	18
South Africa	11	England	5
England	20	South Africa	13
Australia	8	South Africa	5
South Africa	17	Australia	13
New Zealand	15	South Africa	9
South Africa	10	New Zealand	9
Scotland	16	South Africa	7

home sides. Not that anybody believes that referees are objective cheats. It is just hard for referees, in the swell of emotion around a match, to make consistent, rational decisions.

Mallett says: 'Rugby will not progress as long as refereeing controls the destiny of matches.'

For this reason, he is chary of making predictions for the 1999 Rugby World Cup. Too little separates the teams. In 1997-98 England gave South Africa, New Zealand and Australia a run for their money in England. South Africa could well have lost to France in Lyon in 1997. In 1998 there was very little, a kick or two, separating South Africa, New Zealand and Australia in the Tri-Nations matches. South Africa won its four but could easily have lost three of them.

The 1999 Rugby World Cup may well go to the team which is luckiest with refereeing decisions.

THE PLAYERS

Mallett is the selector of his team and the buck for selection stops with him. And he has decided that he wants a team of athletes that can play with continuity to score tries. He has chosen according to that principle and his selections are credible and comprehensible. He has not chopped and changed, believing that a player in the team must be given every opportunity to prove himself. This has given the team the comfort of security.

But on the 1998 tour, one player rocked that sense of security: Bobby Skinstad. He had played so well and was of such high profile that he made some of the established players nervous. Johan Erasmus, André Venter and Gary Teichmann were nervous as they saw him as a rival for their positions. Mark Andrews became nervous as he thought that André Venter could be moved to lock to make room for Skinstad. Mallett had to explain to Erasmus that his place was not in jeopardy. Skinstad was in competition with André Venter for the No. 7 spot, not his place at No. 6 where tackling and playing directly to the ball is more important.

Skinstad had captained Western Province with obvious success, hauling them from the doldrums to the 1998 Currie Cup final. He was an excellent captain of the midweek Springbok side and his own play was outstanding. His success would also cause nervousness amongst aspirant successors to Gary Teichmann for the Springbok captaincy, such as Joost van der Westhuizen and James Dalton.

Eventually Venter was dropped to the bench and Skinstad came in to flank. Mallett believed that Skinstad had a bit more to offer. Venter could tackle like a demon and run well with the ball, but things did not happen off him the way they did off Skinstad. And in any case Venter could tackle and run with the ball just as well as a lock. But for some in the team Bobby Skinstad was an intruder. It was as if the very stability of the team worked against him.

There seems little doubt that Bobby Skinstad, who seems to have worn the glamorous image and the adulation of the Bobby-soxers remarkably well, is the sort of man who could one day do a good job as Springbok captain, representing his country and his team well.

Even in the selection of his Dirt Trackers, Mallett was consistent. He needed an explosive fullback. And so he chose Percy Montgomery as the back-up to Justin Swart in 1997 and Gaffie du Toit as the back-up to Montgomery in 1998.

He wanted physical wings who had pace and were strong on their feet, able to keep the ball alive in a tackle. And so the selections of MacNiel Hendricks in 1997 and Robert Markram in 1998 made sense.

In the centre he needed men who could tackle and when tackled, control the ball. On the 1998 tour he missed Pieter Müller more than he had ever thought he would. But Franco Smith and Christian Stewart looked to fit the bill.

It was not easy to find a successor for Henry Honiball, with his superb defensive abilities and the way he could play in the face of the opposition. Christian Stewart filled a similar rôle for Western Province. Braam van Straaten looked a distinct possibility. But Chad Alcock looked likely to fill the rôle of the game-breaking scrumhalf.

The tight forwards, hooker apart, needed to be athletic and ball players. That is why André Venter appears the ideal lock and why Selborne Boome is so promising. The lock position has not looked secure, though the return of Jan Ackermann, who seemed likely to develop into one of the great tight forwards of the world before his exile, promises much strength.

The hooker has to do his set phases 100 per cent well – throwing in at the line-out and hooking. Andries Truscott may well come into consideration.

The loose-forwards need ball skills and more ball skills. Of course, they have to tackle but above all they have to be able to handle under pressure and with perfect judgement.

Mallett wanted players who could do anything – defend, attack and be disciplined. But he knew that he had tough decisions ahead in 1999. John Hart had stuck with his Incomparables and lost an unprecedented five in a row in 1998. It is harder to drop players when the team is winning.

At the end of 1998 Mallett believed that on defence, always something South Africa did better than anybody else in the world, the Springboks had moved up a step or two. They had won the Tri-Nations on their defence. On attack he believed the Springboks were 20-30 per cent off what they should be.

At the end of a tough but rewarding 1998, Gary Teichmann said: 'Our record speaks for itself. This team still has to reach its full potential. There is no doubt in my mind that the best is still to come. We've got a six-month break and we'll be back stronger than ever.'

THE PLAYERS, A–W

It is incredible to think that in a year 55 Springboks played under Nick Mallett as coach. The following are the Springboks, in alphabetical order, coached by him:

ANDREW DOUGLAS AITKEN
born: Durban, 10 June 1968
test caps: 8
all matches: 10

JAN (JANNIE) HENDRIK DE BEER
born: Welkom, 22 April 1972
test caps: 7
all matches: 8

CHAD DAVID ALCOCK
born: Port Elizabeth, 9 January 1973
test caps: 0
all matches: 4

GERHARDUS MARTHINUS DELPORT
born: Port Elizabeth, 2 February 1975
test caps: 0
all matches: 2

MARK GREGORY ANDREWS
born: Elliot, 21 February 1972
test caps: 53
all matches: 66

ALLEN ERASMUS (NAKA) DROTSKÉ
born: Senekal, 15 March 1971
test caps: 13
all matches: 19

WILLEM WIUM BASSON
born: Paarl, 23 October 1975
test caps: 0
all matches: 2

JACOBUS PETRUS (OS) DU RANDT
born: Elliot, 8 September 1972
test caps: 29
all matches   34

CHRISTOPHER SELBORNE BOOME
born: Somerset West, 16 April 1975
test caps: 0
all matches: 4

GABRIEL STEFANUS (GAFFIE) DU TOIT
born: Cape Town, 24 March 1977
test caps: 1
all matches: 5

WARREN GUY BROSNIHAN
born: Paarl, 28 December 1971
test caps: 1
all matches: 3

WYBRAND WILLEM (BRAAM) ELS
born: Kroonstad, 1 November 1971
test caps: 1
all matches: 3

JAMES DALTON
born: Johannesburg, 16 August 1972
test caps: 34
all matches: 52

JOHAN (RASSIE) ERASMUS
born: Uitenhage, 5 November 1972
test caps: 17
all matches: 20

157

ROBERT (ROBBIE) FRANK FLECK
born: Cape Town, 17 July 1975
test caps: 0
all matches: 4

ANDRÉ-HENRI (OLLIE) LE ROUX
born: Fort Beaufort, 10 May 1973
test caps: 12
all matches: 23

ADRIAN CHRISTOPHER GARVEY
born: Bulawayo, 25 June 1968
test caps: 27
all matches: 27

ROBERT LANCE MARKRAM
born: Kuruman, 5 September 1975
test caps: 0
all matches: 4

JOSEPH (JOE) WILLIAM GILLINGHAM
born: Johannesburg, 27 Feb 1974
test caps: 0
all matches: 7

WILLIE MEYER
born: Port Elizabeth, 6 Nov 1967
test caps: 1
all matches: 5

MacNIEL HENDRICKS
born: Malmesbury, 10 July 1973
test caps: 2
all matches: 4

PERCIVAL (PERCY) COLIN MONTGOMERY
born: Walvis Bay, 15 March 1974
test caps: 22
all matches: 23

HENRY WILLIAM HONIBALL
born: Estcourt, 1 December 1965
test caps: 32
all matches: 42

BRENT SEAN MOYLE
born: Johannesburg, 31 March 1974
test caps: 0
all matches: 1

DEON KAYSER
born: Port Elizabeth, 3 July 1970
test caps: 0
all matches: 4

DICK JOHN MUIR
born: Kokstad, 20 March 1965
test caps: 5
all matches: 10

ROBERT (ROBBIE) KEMPSON
born: Queenstown, 23 January 1974
test caps: 9
all matches: 10

PIETER GYSBERT MÜLLER
born: Bloemfontein, 5 May 1969
test caps: 25
all matches: 39

CORNELIUS JOHANNES PETRUS KRIGE
born: Lusaka, 21 March 1975
test caps: 0
all matches: 4

OWEN SIBUSISO NKUMANE
born: Soweto, 10 August 1975
test caps: 0
all matches: 4

DAVE ROGERS/ALLSPORT

KRYNAUW OTTO
born: Belfast, 8 October 1971
test caps: 24
all matches: 37

Anthem time. The players are Gary Teichmann, Robbie Kempson, James Dalton and Adrian Garvey.

BREYTON JONATHAN PAULSE
born: Ceres, 24 April 1976
test caps: 0
all matches: 8

JAMES TERENCE SMALL
born: Cape Town, 10 February 1969
test caps: 47
all matches: 60

PIETER WILLEM GERHARD ROSSOUW
born: Swellendam, 3 December 1971
test caps: 23
all matches: 23

PHILLIPUS (PHILIP) LODEWICKUS SMIT
born: Burgersdorp, 27 July 1973
test caps: 0
all matches: 5

DALE SANTON
born: Grabouw, 18 August 1969
test caps: 0
all matches: 1

PETRUS FRANCOIS (FRANCO) SMITH
born: Lichtenburg, 29 July 1972
test caps: 8
all matches: 17

ROBERT (BOBBY) BRIAN SKINSTAD
born: Bulawayo, 3 July 1976
test caps: 10
all matches: 14

ANDRIES HENDRIK SNYMAN
born: Newcastle, 2 February 1974
test caps: 29
all matches: 31

JAN CHRISTIAN STEWART
born: Toronto, 17 October 1966
test caps: 3
all matches: 5

JOOST HEYSTEK VAN DER WESTHUIZEN
born: Pretoria, 20 February 1971
test caps: 50
all matches: 68

WERNER SWANEPOEL
born: Bloemfontein, 15 April 1973
test caps: 9
all matches: 13

BRAAM JOHANNES JACOBUS VAN STRAATEN
born: Pretoria, 28 September 1971
test caps: 0
all matches: 4

JUSTIN SWART
born: Stellenbosch, 23 July 1972
test caps: 10
all matches: 12

DANIEL (DAN) JACOBUS VAN ZYL
born: Pretoria, 8 January 1971
test caps: 0
all matches: 1

GARY HAMILTON TEICHMANN
born: Gwelo, 9 January 1967
test caps: 39
all matches: 49

ANDRÉ GERHARDUS VENTER
born: Vereeniging, 14 Nov 1970
test caps: 31
all matches: 33

CARL STEFAN TERBLANCHE
born: Mossel Bay, 2 July 1973
test caps: 12
all matches: 12

SYBRAND LOURENS VENTER
born: Kuruman, 25 June 1976
test caps: 0
all matches: 4

DAVID (DAWIE) FRANCOIS THERON
born: Bloemfontein, 15 Sept1966
test caps: 13
all matches: 13

ANDRÉ NEAL VOS
born: East London, 9 January 1975
test caps: 0
all matches: 4

JOHN (JOHNNY) WILLIAM TRYTSMAN
born: Durbanville, 29 July 1971
test caps: 0
all matches: 4

JOHANNES CONRAAD (BOETA) WESSELS
born: Sishen, 30 June 1973
test caps: 0
all matches: 1

ALBERT (TOKS) VAN DER LINDE
born: Senekal, 30 December 1969
test caps: 6
all matches: 16

CHESTER MORNAY WILLIAMS
born: Paarl, 8 August 1970
test caps: 18
all matches: 31

THE MALLETT MATCHES

SOUTH AFRICA VS ITALY

Stadio Dall'Ara, Bologna, 8 November 1997

Referee:	Pablo Deluca (Argentina)
Touch Judges:	Santiago Borsani (Argentina)
	Marcelo Abdala (Argentina)
Crowd:	20 000
South Africa:	62
Italy:	31
Half-time:	22-20

South Africa: Justin Swart, James Small, André Snyman, Dick Muir, Pieter Rossouw, Henry Honiball, Joost van der Westhuizen, Gary Teichmann (captain), André Venter, Johan Erasmus, Krynauw Otto, Mark Andrews, Adrian Garvey, James Dalton, Piet du Randt
Italy: Javier Pertile (replaced by Massimo Ravazzolo who was replaced by Francesco Mazzariol), Paulo Vaccari, Cristian Stoica, Ivan Francescato, Marcello Cuttita, Diego Dominguez, Alessandro Troncon, Julian Gardner, André Sgorlon, Massimo Giovanelli (captain), Carlo Checchinato (replaced by Walter Cristofoletto), Gianbattista Croci, Franco Properzi Curti, Carlo Orlandi, Massimo Cuttita
SCORERS: **For South Africa:** tries by Rossouw (2), Small (2), Erasmus (2), Du Randt, Swart, Muir; 7 conversions & a penalty goal by Honiball
For Italy: tries by Gardner, Francescato, Vaccari; 2 conversions & 4 penalty goals by Dominguez

This was the last test for Ivan Francescato, of a great Italian rugby family. He died suddenly of heart failure on 20 January 1999.

TERTIUS PICKARD/TOUCHLINE PHOTO AGENCY

Dick Muir making a play against France in 1997 while Henry Honiball backs him up.

SOUTH AFRICA VS BARBARIANS FRANCAISES

Stade Aguilera, Biarritz, 11 November 1997
Referee: Joel Dumé (France)
Touch Judges: Roger Dahau (France)
                  Bernard Pérez (France)

South Africa: 22
French Barbarians: 40
Half-time: 5-17

South Africa: Percy Montgomery, MacNiel Hendricks, Joe Gillingham, Franco Smith, Breyton Paulse (replaced by Thinus Delport), Jannie de Beer, Werner Swanepoel, Andrew Aitken (captain), Philip Smit (replaced by Warren Brosnihan who was replaced by Willie Meyer), Bobby Skinstad, Wium Basson, Braam Els, Dawie Theron, Naka Drotské, Toks van der Linde.
French Barbarians: Nicolas Brusque, Philippe Bernat-Salles (replaced by Marika Vunibaka), David Dantiacq (replaced by Benoit Bellot), Eric Artuguste, Christophe Dominici, Waisale Serevi, Franck Corrihons (replaced by Christophe Laussucq), Mark Lièvremont (replaced by Sylvain Dispagne), Thomas Lièvremont, Serge Betsen, Lagi Matiu (replaced by Sotele Puleoto), Olivier Roumat, Pierre de Villiers, Vincent Moscato (captain), Jean-Jacques Crenca
SCORERS: **For South Africa:** tries by Drotské, Skinstad, Montgomery, De Beer; conversion by De Beer
For French Barbarians: tries by T Lièvremont (2), Matiu, De Villiers, Vunibaka; 3 conversions, 2 penalty goals & a dropped goal by Serevi

SOUTH AFRICA VS FRANCE

Stade Gerland, Lyon, 15 November 1997
Referee: Derek Bevan (Wales)
Touch Judges: Nigel Whitehouse (Wales)
                  Robert Davies (Wales)
Crowd: 25 000

South Africa: 36
France: 32
Half-time: 19-9

South Africa: Percy Montgomery, James Small, André Snyman, Dick Muir, Pieter Rossouw, Henry Honiball, Joost van der Westhuizen (replaced by Werner Swanepoel), Gary Teichmann, André Venter, Johan Erasmus, Krynauw Otto, Mark Andrews, Adrian Garvey, James Dalton, Piet du Randt
France: Jean-Luc Sadourny, Laurent Leflamand, Christophe Lamaison, Stephane Glas, Philippe Saint-André (captain), Thierry Lacroix, Fabien Galthié, Christian Califano, Marc Dal Maso, Franck Tournaire, Olivier Brouzet, Fabien Pelous (replaced by Olivier Merle), Philippe Benetton, Abdelatief Benazzi, Laurent Cabannes
SCORERS: **For South Africa:** tries by Muir, Montgomery, Rossouw, Dalton, Small; 4 conversions & a penalty goal by Honiball
For France: tries by Merle, Califano, Glas; conversion & 5 penalty goals by Lamaison

SOUTH AFRICA VS FRANCE A

Stade Mayol, Toulon, 18 November 1997
Referee: Patrick Thomas (France)
Touch Judges: Gérard Borreani (France)
                     Frank Maciello (France)

South Africa: 7
France A: 21
Half-time: 7-13

South Africa: Thinus Delport, MacNiel Hendricks, Joe Gillingham, Franco Smith, Breyton Paulse, Boeta Wessels, Dan van Zyl, Andrew Aitken (captain), Warren Brosnihan, Bobby Skinstad, Wium Basson (replaced by André Venter, bleeding), Braam Els, Dawie Theron, Dale Santon (replaced by Naka Drotské), Ollie le Roux
France A: Nicolas Brusque (replaced by Philippe Escale), Pierre Bonduoy, Frédéric Leloir, Jean-Marc Aué, David Bory, Benoit Bellot, Pierre Mignoni, Patrick Tabacco, Nicolas Bacqué, Thomas Lièvremont (captain), Hugues Miorin, Thierry Cléda, Richard Crespy, Yannick Bru, Cedric Soulette
SCORERS: **For South Africa:** try by Gillingham; conversion by Smith
For France A: tries by Cléda, Bonduoy; conversion & 3 penalty goals by Bellot

SOUTH AFRICA VS FRANCE

Parc des Princes, Paris, 22 November 1997
Referee: Paddy O'Brien (New Zealand)
Touch Judges: Colin Hawke (New Zealand)
                     Paul Honiss (New Zealand)
Crowd: 56 000

South Africa: 52
France: 10
Half-time: 28-3

South Africa: Percy Montgomery, James Small, André Snyman, Dick Muir, Pieter Rossouw (replaced by Jannie de Beer), Henry Honiball, Werner Swanepoel, Joost van der Westhuizen, Gary Teichmann (captain), André Venter, Johan Erasmus (replaced by Andrew Aitken), Krynauw Otto, Mark Andrews, Adrian Garvey, James Dalton, Piet du Randt
France: Jean-Luc Sadourny, David Venditti (replaced by Laurent Leflamand), Christophe Lamaison (replaced by Thierry Lacroix), Stephane Glas, Philippe Saint-André (captain) (replaced by Philippe Benetton), Thierry Lacroix (replaced by David Aucagne), Fabien Galthié (replaced by Jérôme Cazalbou who was replaced by Christophe Lamaison), Christian Califano, Marc Dal Maso (replaced by Raphaël Ibañez), Franck Tournaire, Olivier Brouzet, Olivier Merle, Philippe Benetton (replaced by Didier Casadéi)
SCORERS: **For South Africa:** tries by Rossouw (4), Snyman, Teichmann, Honiball; 7 conversions & a penalty goal by Honiball
For France: try by Ibañez; conversion & penalty goal by Lamaison

SOUTH AFRICA VS ENGLAND

Twickenham, London, 29 November 1997

Referee:	Colin Hawke (New Zealand)
Touch Judges:	Paddy O'Brien (New Zealand)
	Paul Honiss (New Zealand)
Crowd:	71 000

South Africa:	28
England:	11
Half-time:	7-11

South Africa: Percy Montgomery, James Small, André Snyman, Dick Muir, Pieter Rossouw, Henry Honiball, Werner Swanepoel, Joost van der Westhuizen, Gary Teichmann (captain), André Venter (temporarily replaced by Bobby Skinstad), Andrew Aitken, Krynauw Otto, Mark Andrews, Adrian Garvey, James Dalton, Piet du Randt

England: Matt Perry, John Bentley (replaced by Austin Healey), Will Greenwood, Nick Greenstock, David Rees, Mike Catt (replaced by Paul Grayson), Matt Dawson, Richard Hill (replaced by Chris Sheasby), Neil Back, Lawrence Dallaglio (captain), Danny Grewcock (replaced by Simon Shaw), Garath Archer, Darren Garforth, Richard Cockerill, Jason Leonard

SCORERS: **For South Africa:** tries by Garvey, Snyman, Andrews, Swanepoel; 2 conversions & penalty by Honiball; conversion by Montgomery

For England: try by Greenstock; 2 penalty goals by Catt

SOUTH AFRICA VS SCOTLAND

Murrayfield, Edinburgh, 6 December 1997

Referee:	Patrick Thomas (France)
Touch Judges:	Joel Dumé (France)
	Roger Duhau (France)
Crowd:	30 000

South Africa:	68
Scotland:	10
Half-time:	14-3

South Africa: Percy Montgomery, James Small (replaced by Justin Swart), André Snyman, Dick Muir, Pieter Rossouw, Jannie de Beer (replaced by Franco Smith), Werner Swanepoel), Gary Teichmann (captain), André Venter, Johan Erasmus, Krynauw Otto, Mark Andrews, Adrian Garvey, James Dalton, Piet du Randt (replaced by Willie Meyer)

Scotland: Rowen Shepherd, Craig Joiner, Tony Stanger, Craig Chalmers (replaced by Duncan Hodge), Derek Stark, Gregor Townsend, Andy Nicol (replaced by Gary Armstrong), Eric Peters (replaced by Peter Walton), Ian Smith, Rob Wainwright (captain), Stewart Campbell, Scott Murray, Mattie Stewart, Gordon Bulloch, David Hilton (replaced by George Graham)

SCORERS: **For South Africa:** tries by Montgomery (2), Small (2), Erasmus, Rossouw, Teichmann, Venter, Snyman, Smith; 8 conversions by Montgomery; conversion by De Beer

For Scotland: try by Stark; conversion & penalty goal by Shepherd

SOUTH AFRICA VS IRELAND
Free State Stadium, Bloemfontein, 13 June 1998

Referee:	Ed Morrison (England)
Touch Judges:	Joel Dumé (France)
	Didier Méné (France)
Crowd:	25 000
South Africa:	37
Ireland:	13
Half-time:	13-10

1998 1998 1998

South Africa: Percy Montgomery, Stefan Terblanche, André Snyman, Pieter Müller, Pieter Rossouw, Gaffie du Toit (temporarily replaced by Franco Smith), Joost van der Westhuizen, Gary Teichmann (captain), André Venter, Johan Erasmus, Krynauw Otto, Mark Andrews, Adrian Garvey, James Dalton, Ollie le Roux
Ireland: Conor O'Shea, Justin Bishop (replaced by Rob Henderson), Kevin Maggs, Mark McCall, Denis Hickie (replaced by Rob Henderson), Eric Elwood, Conor McGuinness, Victor Costello (replaced by Trevor Brennan), Andy Ward, Dion O'Cuinneagain (replaced by Trevor Brennan), Malcolm O'Kelly, Paddy Johns (captain) (replaced by Gabriel Fulcher), Paul Wallace, Keith Wood, Justin Fitzpatrick
SCORERS: **For South Africa:** tries by Terblanche (4), Andrews; 3 conversions & 2 penalty goals by Du Toit
For Ireland: try by Bishop; conversion & 2 penalty goals by Elwood

SOUTH AFRICA VS IRELAND
Loftus Versfeld, Pretoria, 20 June 1998

Referee:	Joel Dumé (France)
Touch Judges:	Ed Morrison (England)
	Didier Méné (France)
Crowd:	25 000
South Africa:	33
Ireland:	0
Half-time:	19-0

South Africa: Percy Montgomery, Stefan Terblanche (replaced by MacNiel Hendricks), André Snyman, Pieter Müller, Pieter Rossouw, Henry Honiball, Joost van der Westhuizen (replaced by Werner Swanepoel), Gary Teichmann (captain), André Venter, Johan Erasmus (replaced by Andrew Aitken), Krynauw Otto, Mark Andrews, Adrian Garvey (replaced by Ollie le Roux), James Dalton (replaced by Naka Drotské), Ollie le Roux (replaced by Robbie Kempson)
Ireland: Conor O'Shea, Justin Bishop, Kevin Maggs, Mark McCall, Denis Hickie (replaced by Rob Henderson), Eric Elwood (replaced by David Humphreys), Conor McGuinness, Victor Costello (replaced by Trevor Brennan), Andy Ward, Dion O'Cuinneagain (replaced by Trevor Brennan), Malcolm O'Kelly , Paddy Johns (captain) (replaced by Gabriel Fulcher), Paul Wallace, Keith Wood, Justin Fitzpatrick (replaced by Peter Clohessy)
SCORERS: **For South Africa:** tries by Terblanche, Rossouw, Van der Westhuizen, Teichmann, Erasmus, Dalton; 4 conversions by Montgomery

SOUTH AFRICA VS WALES

Loftus Versfeld, Pretoria, 27 June 1998

Referee: Paddy O'Brien, New Zealand)
Touch Judges: Colin Hawke (New Zealand)
                  David McHugh (Ireland)
Crowd: 33 000

South Africa: 96
Wales: 13
Half-time: 31-6

South Africa: Percy Montgomery, Stefan Terblanche (replaced by MacNiel Hendricks), André Snyman, Pieter Müller (replaced by Franco Smith), Pieter Rossouw, Franco Smith (replaced by Henry Honiball), Joost van der Westhuizen (replaced by Werner Swanepoel), Gary Teichmann (captain) (replaced by Andrew Aitken), André Venter, Johan Erasmus, Krynauw Otto, Mark Andrews (replaced by Bobby Skinstad), Adrian Garvey (replaced by Ollie le Roux), James Dalton (replaced by Naka Drotské), Robbie Kempson
Wales: Byron Hayward (replaced by Darril Williams), Dafydd James, Mark Taylor, John Funnell (replaced by Stephen Jones), Garan Evans, Arwel Thomas, Paul John (replaced by David Llewellyn), Colin Charvis (replaced by Geraint Lewis), Kingsley Jones (captain) (replaced by Chris Wyatt), Nathan Thomas, Andrew Moore, Ian Gough, John Davies (replaced by Darren Morris), Barry Williams (replaced by Garin Jenkins), Mike Griffiths
SCORERS: **For South Africa:** tries by Montgomery (2), Terblanche (2), Rossouw (3), Smith, Van der Westhuizen, Venter (2), Erasmus, Otto, Hendricks, Skinstad; 9 conversions & a penalty goal by Montgomery
For Wales: try by Thomas; conversion & 2 penalty goals by Thomas

SOUTH AFRICA VS ENGLAND

Newlands, Cape Town, 4 July 1998

Referee: Colin Hawke (New Zealand)
Touch Judges: Paddy O'Brien (New Zealand)
                 David McHugh (Ireland)
Crowd: 40 000

South Africa: 18
England: 0
Half-time: 12-0

South Africa: Percy Montgomery, Stefan Terblanche, André Snyman, Pieter Müller, Pieter Rossouw, Henry Honiball, Joost van der Westhuizen, Gary Teichmann (captain), André Venter, Johan Erasmus, Krynauw Otto (temporarily replaced by Bobby Skinstad), Mark Andrews, Adrian Garvey (replaced by Ollie le Roux), James Dalton, Robbie Kempson (replaced by Ollie le Roux)
England: Matt Perry, Spencer Brown, Nick Beal, Jos Baxendell, Paul Sampson (replaced by Tim Stimpson), Josh Lewsey, Matt Dawson (captain), Tony Diprose, Pat Sanderson, Ben Clarke, Dave Sims, Rob Fidler, Phil Vickery, Richard Cockerill, Graham Rowntree
SCORERS: **For South Africa:** tries by Van der Westhuizen & Terblanche; conversion & 2 penalty goals by Montgomery

SOUTH AFRICA VS AUSTRALIA
Subiaco Oval, Perth, 18 July 1998
Referee:	Colin Hawke (New Zealand)
Touch Judges:	Paddy O'Brien (New Zealand)
	Clayton Thomas (Wales)
Crowd: 38 079	

South Africa:	14
Australia:	13
Half-time:	8-8

South Africa: Percy Montgomery (temporarily replaced by Chester Williams), Stefan Terblanche, André Snyman, Pieter Müller, Pieter Rossouw, Henry Honiball, Joost van der Westhuizen, Gary Teichmann (captain), André Venter, Johan Erasmus, Krynauw Otto, Mark Andrews, Adrian Garvey (replaced by Ollie le Roux), James Dalton, Robbie Kempson (replaced by Ollie le Roux)
Australia: Matt Burke, Ben Tune (replaced by Damian Smith), Daniel Herbert, Tim Horan, Joe Roff, Stephen Larkham, George Gregan, Totai Kefu (replaced by Willie Ofahengaue), David Wilson, Matt Cockbain (temporarily replaced by Owen Finegan), John Eales (captain), Tom Bowman, Andrew Blades, Phil Kearns (temporarily replaced by Jeremy Paul), Dan Crowley
SCORERS: **For South Africa:** try by Van der Westhuizen; 3 penalty goals by Montgomery
For Australia: tries by Tune & Gregan; penalty goal by Burke

SOUTH AFRICA VS NEW ZEALAND
Athletic Park, Wellington, 25 July 1998
Referee:	Ed Morrison (England)
Touch Judges:	Derek Bevan (Wales)
	Brian Campsall (England)
Crowd:	40 000

South Africa:	13
New Zealand:	3
Half-time:	3-0

South Africa: Percy Montgomery, Stefan Terblanche, André Snyman (replaced by Franco Smith), Pieter Müller, Pieter Rossouw (temporarily replaced by Chester Williams), Henry Honiball, Joost van der Westhuizen, Gary Teichmann (captain), André Venter, Johan Erasmus, Krynauw Otto, Mark Andrews (replaced by Bobby Skinstad), Adrian Garvey (replaced by Ollie le Roux), James Dalton, Robbie Kempson (replaced by Ollie le Roux)
New Zealand: Christian Cullen, Jeff Wilson, Mark Mayerhofler (replaced by Scott McLeod), Walter Little, Jonah Lomu, Carlos Spencer (replaced by Andrew Mehrtens), Justin Marshall (replaced by Ofisa Tonu'u), Taine Randell (captain), Josh Kronfeld, Michael Jones (replaced by Isitolo Maka), Robin Brooke, Ian Jones, Olo Brown, Anton Oliver, Craig Dowd
SCORERS: **For South Africa:** try by Pieter Rossouw; conversion & 2 penalty goals by Montgomery
For New Zealand: penalty goal by Mehrtens

SOUTH AFRICA vs NEW ZEALAND

King's Park, Durban, 15 August 1998

Referee:	Peter Marshall (Australia)
Touch Judges:	Wayne Erickson (Australia)
	Jim Fleming (Scotland)
Crowd:	51 000

South Africa:	24
New Zealand:	23
Half-time:	5-17

South Africa: Percy Montgomery, Stefan Terblanche, André Snyman (replaced by Franco Smith), Pieter Müller, Pieter Rossouw, Henry Honiball, Joost van der Westhuizen, Gary Teichmann (captain), André Venter, Johan Erasmus (replaced by Andrew Aitken), Krynauw Otto (replaced by Bobby Skinstad), Mark Andrews (replaced by Krynauw Otto), Adrian Garvey (replaced by Ollie le Roux), James Dalton, Robbie Kempson
New Zealand: Christian Cullen, Jeff Wilson, Eroni Clarke (replaced by Norm Berryman), Mark Mayerhofler, Walter Little, Jonah Lomu, Andrew Mehrtens, Justin Marshall, Isitolo Maka (replaced by Scott Robertson), John Kronfeld, Taine Randell (captain), Robin Brooke, Royce Willis, Olo Brown, Anton Oliver, Carl Hoeft
SCORERS: **For South Africa:** tries by Terblanche, Skinstad, Van der Westhuizen, Dalton; 2 conversions by Montgomery
For New Zealand: tries by Marshall & Randell; 2 conversions, 3 penalty goals by Mehrtens

SOUTH AFRICA vs AUSTRALIA

Ellis Park, Johannesburg, 22 August 1998

Referee:	Jim Fleming (Scotland)
Touch Judges:	Joel Dumé (France)
	David McHugh (Ireland)
Crowd:	62 308

South Africa:	29
Australia:	15
Half-time:	16-12

South Africa: Percy Montgomery, Stefan Terblanche, André Snyman (replaced by Franco Smith), Pieter Müller, Pieter Rossouw, Henry Honiball, Joost van der Westhuizen, Gary Teichmann (captain), André Venter, Johan Erasmus (replaced by Andrew Aitken), Krynauw Otto, Mark Andrews (replaced by Bobby Skinstad who went to flank while Venter moved to lock), Adrian Garvey, James Dalton, Robbie Kempson (replaced by Ollie le Roux)
Australia: Matt Burke, Ben Tune (replaced by Nathan Grey) Daniel Herbert (replaced by Jason Little), Tim Horan, Joe Roff, Stephen Larkham (replaced by Chris Whitaker), George Gregan, Totai Kefu (replaced by Willie Ofahengaue), David Wilson, Matt Cockbain (replaced by Owen Finegan), Tom Bowman, John Eales, Andrew Blades (replaced by Glen Panoho), Phil Kearns, Dan Crowley
SCORERS: **For South Africa:** tries by Garvey & Skinstad; 2 conversions & 5 penalty goals by Montgomery
For Australia: 5 penalty goals by Burke

SOUTH AFRICA VS GLASGOW CALEDONIANS

Firhill Stadium, Glasgow, 7 pm (GMT), 10 November 1998

Referee:	Nigel Whitehouse (Wales)
Touch Judges:	Robert Davies (Wales)
	Huw Lewis (Wales)
Crowd:	2 500 (capacity: 19 000)

South Africa:	62
Glasgow Caledonians:	9
Half-time:	26-9

South Africa: Gaffie du Toit, Lourens Venter (replaced by Deon Kayser), Robbie Fleck, Christian Stewart, Breyton Paulse, Braam van Straaten (replaced by Robert Markram, who went to fullback with Du Toit moving to flyhalf), Werner Swanepoel (replaced by Chad Alcock), Bobby Skinstad (captain), André Vos, Corné Krige, Johnny Trytsman, Selborne Boome (replaced by Philip Smit), Willie Meyer, Naka Drotské (replaced by Owen Nkumane), Ollie le Roux (replaced by Toks van der Linde)
Glasgow Caledonians: Tommy Hayes, James Craig (replaced by Alan Bulloch), Ian Jardine, John Leslie, Derek Stark, Luke Smith, Derrick Patterson, Gordon McKay, John Shaw (captain) (replaced by Gareth Flockhart), Jason White, Guy Perrett, Stewart Campbell, Alan Little, Kevin McKenzie (replaced by Gavin Scott), Gordon McIlwham
SCORERS: For South Africa: tries by Boome, Paulse (3), Fleck (2), Venter, Du Toit, Van Straaten, Skinstad; conversions by Van Straaten (6)
For Glasgow Caledonians: penalties by Tommy Hayes (3)

SOUTH AFRICA VS WALES

**Wembley Stadium, London, 3 pm (GMT),
14 November 1998**

Referee:	Stuart Dickinson (Australia)
Touch Judges:	Ed Morrison (England)
	Jim Fleming (Scotland)
Crowd:	51 350 (capacity: 79 000)

South Africa:	28
Wales:	20
Half-time:	14-14

South Africa: Percy Montgomery, Stefan Terblanche, André Snyman, Franco Smith, Pieter Rossouw, Henry Honiball, Joost van der Westhuizen, Gary Teichmann (captain), André Venter, Johan Erasmus, Krynauw Otto, Mark Andrews (replaced by Bobby Skinstad), Adrian Garvey (replaced by Ollie le Roux), James Dalton, Robbie Kempson
Wales: Shane Howarth, Gareth Thomas, Mark Taylor, Scott Gibbs, Dafydd James, Neil Jenkins, Robert Howley (captain), Scott Quinnell, Martyn Williams, Colin Charvis, Chris Wyatt, Craig Quinnell, Chris Anthony (replaced by Ben Evans), Jonathan Humphreys, Andrew Lewis (replaced by Darren Morris)
SCORERS: For South Africa: tries by Van der Westhuizen & Venter; penalty try; 2 conversions & 3 penalty goals by Smith
For Wales: try by Gareth Thomas; 5 penalty goals by Neil Jenkins

169

SOUTH AFRICA VS EDINBURGH REIVERS

Easter Road Stadium, Edinburgh, 7 pm (GMT), 17 November 1998

Referee:	Murray Whyte (Ireland)
Touch Judges:	Gordon Black (Ireland)
	Eddie Walsh (Ireland)
Crowd:	1 463 (capacity: 16 000)

South Africa:	49
Edinburgh Reivers:	3
Half-time:	21-3

South Africa: Breyton Paulse (replaced by Gaffie du Toit), Robert Markram, Robbie Fleck, Braam van Straaten, Deon Kayser, Christian Stewart (replaced by Lourens Venter), Chad Alcock (replaced by Werner Swanepoel), Bobby Skinstad (captain) (replaced by Johnny Trytsman), André Vos, Corné Krige, Philip Smit, Selborne Boome, Willie Meyer, Owen Nkumane (replaced by Naka Drotské), Toks van der Linde (replaced by Ollie le Roux)
Edinburgh Reivers: Stuart Lang, Hugh Gilmour, Scott Hastings, Iain Fairley, John Kerr (replaced by Alistair Common), Scott Welsh (replaced by G Ross), Graeme Burns, Brian Renwick (captain), Iain Sinclair, Adam Roxburgh (replaced by Carl Hogg), Iain Fullarton, Darren Burns (replaced by Thomas McVie), Barry Stewart, Stephen Scott (replaced by Jim Hay), Ross McNulty (replaced by Peter Wright)
SCORERS: **For South Africa:** tries by Van der Linde, Vos, Skinstad, Le Roux, Meyer, Krige, Venter; conversions by Van Straaten (7)
For Edinburgh Reivers: penalty by Welsh

SOUTH AFRICA VS SCOTLAND

Murrayfield, Edinburgh, 3 pm (GMT), 21 November 1998

Referee:	Nigel White (England)
Touch Judges:	Peter Marshall (Australia)
	Scott Young (Australia)
Crowd:	29 765 (capacity: 68 000)

South Africa:	35
Scotland:	10
Half-time:	11-7

South Africa: Percy Montgomery, Stefan Terblanche, André Snyman, Christian Stewart, Pieter Rossouw, Henry Honiball, Joost van der Westhuizen, Gary Teichmann (captain), Bobby Skinstad, Johan Erasmus, Krynauw Otto (replaced by André Venter), Mark Andrews, Adrian Garvey (replaced by Ollie le Roux), James Dalton, Robbie Kempson
Scotland: Derrick Lee (replaced by Gregor Townsend), Alan Tait (replaced by Kenny Logan), Jamie Mayer, John Leslie, Cameron Murray, Duncan Hodge, Bryan Redpath (captain) (replaced by Gary Armstrong), Eric Peters, Budge Poutney, Peter Walton (replaced by Martin Leslie), Doddie Weir, Scott Murray, Paul Burnell (replaced by David Hilton), Gordon Bulloch, Tom Smith
SCORERS: **For South Africa:** tries by Terblanche, Van der Westhuizen, Snyman, Rossouw, Skinstad; 2 penalties and 2 conversions by Montgomery
For Scotland: try, conversion & penalty by Hodge

SOUTH AFRICA VS COMBINED IRISH PROVINCES

Musgrave Park, Cork, 7 pm (GMT), 24 November 1998

Referee:	Frank Maciello (France)
Touch Judges:	Frank Florens (France)
	Jean-Pierre Matheu (France)
Crowd:	8 000

South Africa:	32
Combined Provinces:	5
Half-time:	15-0

South Africa: Gaffie du Toit, Lourens Venter, Robbie Fleck, Franco Smith (replaced by Deon Kayser), Breyton Paulse, Braam van Straaten (replaced by Robert Markram), Werner Swanepoel (replaced by Chad Alcock), André Vos (captain), Phillip Smit, André Venter, Johnny Trytsman, Selborne Boome, Willie Meyer, Naka Drotské (replaced by Owen Nkumane), Toks van der Linde (replaced by Ollie le Roux)
Combined Provinces: Ciaran Clarke (replaced by Simon Mason), John Kelly (replaced by Sean Horgan), Killian Keane, Mervin Murphy, Jan Cunningham, Barry Everett, Stephen Bell (replaced by Peter Stringer), Anthony Foley (replaced by Declan O'Brien), Eddie Halvey, David Wallace, Jimmy Duffy (replaced by Gary Longwell), Mick Galwey (captain), John Hayes (replaced by Des Clohessy), Alan Clarke (replaced by Sean Byrne), Emmet Byrne,
SCORERS: For South Africa: tries by André Venter, Van Straaten, Paulse (2), Ollie le Roux; 2 conversions, 1 penalty by Van Straaten
For Combined Provinces: try by Halvey

SOUTH AFRICA VS IRELAND

Lansdowne Road, Dublin, 3 pm (GMT), 28 November 1998

Referee:	Clayton Thomas (Wales)
Touch Judges:	Ed Morrison (England)
	Jim Fleming (Scotland)
Crowd:	48 000

South Africa:	27
Ireland:	13
Half-time:	7-6

South Africa: Percy Montgomery, Stefan Terblanche, André Snyman, Christian Stewart, Pieter Rossouw, Henry Honiball, Joost van der Westhuizen, Gary Teichmann (captain), Bobby Skinstad, Johan Erasmus, Krynauw Otto, Mark Andrews (replaced by André Venter), Adrian Garvey, James Dalton (replaced by Naka Drotské), Robbie Kempson (replaced by Ollie le Roux who was in turn replaced by Kempson)
Ireland: Conor O'Shea, Justin Bishop, Kevin Maggs, Jonathan Bell, Girvan Dempsey, Eric Elwood, Conor McGuinness, Victor Costello, Andy Ward, Dion O'Cuinneagain, Malcolm O'Kelly (replaced by Jeremy Davidson), Paddy Johns (captain), Peter Clohessy, Keith Wood (replaced by Ross Nesdale), Justin Fitzpatrick (replaced by Reggie Corrigan)
SCORERS: For South Africa: tries by Erasmus, Skinstad, Van der Westhuizen; 3 conversions & 2 penalty goals by Montgomery
For Ireland: try by Wood; conversion and 2 penalty goals by Elwood

SOUTH AFRICA VS IRELAND A
Ravenhill, Belfast, 7.30 pm (GMT), 1 December 1998
Referee: Rob Dickson (Scotland)
Touch Judges: Chuck Muir (Scotland)
Jim Johnston (Scotland)
Crowd: 9 000

South Africa: 50
Ireland A: 19
Half-time: 19-9

South Africa: Gaffie du Toit, Robert Markram (replaced by Breyton Paulse), Robbie Fleck, Franco Smith (replaced by Lourens Venter), Deon Kayser, Braam van Straaten, Chad Alcock (replaced by Werner Swanepoel), André Vos (captain), Corné Krige, Phillip Smit, André Venter (replaced by Selborne Boome), Johnny Trytsman, Brent Moyle, Owen Nkumane (replaced by Ollie le Roux), Toks van der Linde
Ireland A: Girvan Dempsey, Niall Woods (replaced by Simon Mason), Rob Henderson, Pat Duigan, Darragh O'Mahony, David Humphreys, Ciaran Scally, Anthony Foley, Eddie Halvey (replaced by David Wallace), David Corkery, Jeremy Davidson (replaced by Jimmy Duffy), Mick Galwey (captain), John Hayes (replaced by Emmet Byrne), Ross Nesdale (replaced by Alan Clarke), Reggie Corrigan
SCORERS: **For South Africa:** tries by Fleck, Alcock, Du Toit (2), Smith, Van Straaten, Lourens Venter, Swanepoel; 5 conversions by Van Straaten
For Ireland A: try by O'Mahony; conversion by Mason, & 4 penalty goals by Woods

SOUTH AFRICA VS ENGLAND
Twickenham, London, 5 December 1998
Referee: Paddy O'Brien (New Zealand)
Touch Judges: Jim Fleming (Scotland)
Paul Honiss (New Zealand)
Crowd: 75 000

South Africa: 7
England: 13
Half-time: 7-7

South Africa: Percy Montgomery, Stefan Terblanche, André Snyman, Christian Stewart, Pieter Rossouw, Henry Honiball, Joost van der Westhuizen (replaced by Werner Swanepoel), Gary Teichmann (captain), Bobby Skinstad, Johan Erasmus, Krynauw Otto, Mark Andrews (replaced by André Venter), Adrian Garvey (replaced by Ollie le Roux), James Dalton, Robbie Kempson (replaced by Ollie le Roux for bleeding)
England: Nick Beal, Tony Underwood (replaced by David Rees who was replaced by Austin Healey), Jeremy Guscott, Phil de Glanville (replaced by Alex King), Dan Luger, Mike Catt (temporarily replaced by Martin Corry), Matt Dawson, Richard Hill, Neil Back, Lawrence Dallaglio (captain), Tim Rodber (replaced by Danny Grewcock), Martin Johnson, Darren Garforth, Richard Cockerill, Jason Leonard
SCORERS: **For South Africa:** try by Rossouw; conversion by Montgomery
For England: try by Guscott; conversion & 2 penalty goals by Dawson

INDEX